Dating

Avoiding Hell on Earth
2nd Edition 2013

Jeff Mullins

Cover Photo: The collage is composed of pictures at the weddings of the author's children. These include three pictures from each wedding plus two family pictures.

Second Edition

ISBN-13:
978-1490483351

ISBN-10:
1490483357

Additional copies of this, or the author's other books, are available at amazon.com.

DEDICATION

Dedicated to Hannah, Katie, Bethany, Micaiah, Kara Joy, Malia and Luke, the beloved children who were entrusted to my wife Mary and me.

With profound gratitude to God for my wonderful wife, Mary, the mother of our children.

With joy and faith that God may use the offering of this work to His glory as a minuscule token of appreciation for His immeasurable love and gift of salvation.

CONTENTS

ACKNOWLEDGMENTS

By the grace of God, I have been blessed with opportunities to help those committed to godly marriages navigate their way through rough waters. There have been some successes and many lessons learn along the way.

Unfortunately, I have also been witness to many marriages that have been destroyed upon the reefs, shoals and rocks of selfishness, pride and inconsideration. This has also been instructive.

God, by His grace, has provided me with a wife committed to lifelong marriage and willing to work through the issues of life as they arise. Through these experiences I have learned much. I am still learning. God has also entrusted me with seven wonderful children who may someday be married. My concern for them and their marriages has been a great impetus to write this book.

These experiences are the backdrop for this book. It is offered with the hope that God will use it to help someone avoid the pain and heartache of a bad or broken marriage.

I am under no illusion that this book is the final word on the topic. Neither do I offer an expert opinion. Rather, the following pages simply attempt to apply the teaching of the truth of God from a straightforward reading of the Bible where it intersects with the daily grind of married life.

INTRODUCTION

Although neither heaven nor hell exist on this earth, some experiences are so painful that some people imagine them to constitute "hell on earth." We can be sure of two things:

1. True hell is unimaginable. The suffering, agony and pain of hell can in no way be compared to this earthly life's experiences, and

2. This life's suffering, pain and agony is seemingly so unbearable at times it is hard to imagine something worse.

Sometimes the suffering arises from events and circumstances beyond an individual's control and completely apart from their actions. However, in other instances, individual attitudes, choices and actions bring consequences that are clearly a self inflicted "hell on earth."

Since each person has control over their own attitudes and actions, many of life's troubles can be avoided. This book offers help in avoiding trouble in dating and marriage. God created marriage and concluded that it was very good. When God is followed, marriage can be more like heaven than hell.

Marriage offers potential heavenly bliss or a hellish nightmare. Marriage may be the source of one's greatest joy in life or the heaviest burden in life. To a significant degree, the difference depends upon who you choose as your life-long spouse. Second only to trusting in Jesus for eternal salvation, deciding who to marry is the most weighty decision any person will ever make. Ironically, the choice of who to marry is often made by relatively immature people who are strongly influenced by emotions and hormones rather than by reason and reflection.

Many of the problems in existing marriages are the direct result of a dating process that was inadequate, unfocused and faulty. The saying "An ounce of prevention is worth a pound of cure" is applicable to dating and marriage. Consequently, hope for successful marriages is found in an intentional approach to dating. Using the Bible as a guide, dating will be assessed and evaluated in the following pages. Suggestions are offered to provoke thought about the process of dating, the purpose of dating and the practices of dating. The reader can expect their assumptions about dating to be challenged, increasing the likelihood of experiencing marital success.

An underlying premise of this book is a straightforward approach to interpreting of the Bible. The assumption is that the Creator knows His creatures better than any psychologist, psychiatrist or philosopher. God knows our nature, our needs and the solutions to our problems. God also has the authority to tell us what is right and what is wrong. He has the power to change lives.

Fortunately, God has provided specific instructions and principles to help us understand the marriage relationship. There are not specific biblical instructions about dating. But understanding the role of dating, as it relates to what the Bible teaches about marriage, will enable an approach to dating that is clearly based on the teachings of the Bible.

Many of the issues raised in the pages that follow are to provoke thoughtful consideration. The assumption is that the reader truly seeks biblical truth and does not need to be overwhelmed with proofs to be convinced of the truth.

<u>Addressed to Christians</u>

Although anyone who understands and applies the truths of the Bible to his life will benefit, this book is primarily for those who are Christians. What does it mean to be a Christian? Who is a Christian?

A Christian is one who has been reconciled to God through personal faith in Jesus Christ as his Lord and Savior. This includes:
- acknowledging personal sin and guilt that separates each one from God.
- knowing that Jesus is fully God and fully man.
- believing that Jesus died on the cross and that He forever lives, having physically risen from the dead.
- trusting in Jesus alone, apart from personal merit or works for forgiveness of sins and salvation unto eternal life

God grants salvation and eternal life as a gift to the one who believes in Jesus, who said,

> "Truly, truly, I say to you, he who hears My word, and believes Him who sent Me, has eternal life, and does not come into judgment, but has passed out of death into life."[1]

The judgment referred to in the above text is eternal hell – separation from God in a place the Bible calls the Lake of Fire.[2] **Finding peace with God through faith in Jesus Christ is the most important thing in life** because it matters for eternity. Achieving harmony and peace in marriage is secondary to salvation

---

1 John 5:24

2   Revelation 20:10-15

because, although it is very significant, it is an earthly relationship that lasts only for a time.

May God bless you as you consider dating and marriage. May God grant you the grace to avoid relationships which may create your very own "hell on earth" in dating or in marriage. May He give you wisdom to make choices that will please Him and make life pleasant for you.

Although dating comes before marriage in life, marriage will be discussed first in this book. This is because understanding marriage is a prerequisite to gaining a proper view of dating.

To facilitate use in youth groups or Sunday School classes, study questions have been included in an appendix. Please feel free to photocopy these questions.

If you are already married it is likely that the following pages will provide clarity in your marriage and encouragement to be the spouse you should be. Praise be to God, if this book helps you.

A Word about Parents

It is natural that parents view their children dating differently than they viewed it for themselves. Life's experiences have taught parents many lessons by the time their own children approach dating age. Parents know first hand (for good or for bad) that choosing whom to marry is one of the most important decisions that their child will make. And contrary to how children sometimes think, parents want good things for their children. Devoted parents often quiver at the thought of their children making decisions about dating and marriage that may bring great and lasting pain into their children's lives.

Like their children, parents have questions too:
- Who will my child marry?
- How will they meet them?
- Will they be able to avoid the mistakes that I made?
- How can I help them through this transition?
- What are my responsibilities to my children regarding dating?
- Can I ensure that they will be careful to choose a good mate?
- Have I given them what they need to make good choices?

As the father of seven children, it is has been my desire that each child find a spouse who will be faithful to them and committed to God all the days of their life. As a pastor who has witnessed shattered lives, spoiled relationships, and fractured homes, it breaks my heart to think that the future may hold some of these for my own children. I feel a great burden of responsibility to help my own children, as well as others, regarding understanding dating and marriage. For this reason I have written this book.

When it was first published in 1999, this book was part of my continuing effort to educate my children in the ways of the Lord. I was compelled to put into writing many of the concepts that I had tried to teach them throughout their developmental years. By putting these things in print it was my hope that they would have a ready resource for years to come. I have sought to present God as the authority, recognizing that my children ultimately belong to Him and are accountable to Him. At the same time, I have shared numerous personal experiences and observations. Hopefully, others will be able to profit from this work as well.

Please consider this book as one father's attempt to teach his own children about dating and marriage with the hope that they will avoid some of the many heartaches so many people experience.

Introduction to 2nd Edition

When writing the 1st edition my oldest daughter was 16 years old, and of course, at that age, none of my children were married. Now, fourteen years later, three of my children are married.

All of my seven children have read this book under compulsion. Several of them have voluntarily reread it numerous times as events in their own lives, and the lives of others, spurred them to do so. I wish I could say that the instructions provided in these pages have been embraced by all my children, but I cannot. As they have entered adulthood each child has made their own decisions, for good or for bad.

The second edition has been updated and extensively revised based on another decade of life experience and increased insight into God's Word. Some of the material has been reorganized. Three completely new chapters have been added:
- "Attraction, Modesty and Flirting"
- "How to Find a Husband or Wife"
- "The Wedding"

May God bless you abundantly and give you a heart to love and obey Him. May your dating and marriage experiences be pleasant to you and pleasing to God.

Sincerely by God's grace,

Pastor Jeff

Chapter 1
Origin And Definition Of Marriage!
Whose Idea Is It Anyway?

He who finds a wife finds a good thing, and obtains favor from the LORD.
(Proverbs 18:22)

A Sad Story

Sam sat at the kitchen table with his face perched in his hands. Dark bags under his eyes hid behind clammy palms. He did not know how long he had been there. He did not care. An oily film floated on the surface of his half full cup of coffee. The toast which he had made for breakfast had become stale. His racing mind was strangely blank. Emotions flooded his empty soul. Nothing seemed real except his confusion, hopelessness and despair.

All that was previously so important now seemed irrelevant. Long hours invested to ensure success meant nothing. The prosperity of his business was now insignificant. Having a beautiful home built with his own two hands was as worthless as a small tent. He no longer cared about that. Savings accounts, investments, and retirement planning added up to nothing. Nothing mattered now but one thing . . .

The grandfather clock chimed out a distant reckoning of the hour. Sam peered between his fingers. It was ten a.m. It had seemed like only minutes. Four hours had passed. It felt like an instant and an eternity at the same time. He did not care. His business should have opened two hours ago, but it did not. Customers would be waiting, but what did it matter? Nothing seemed to matter. The hollow ticking of the clock echoed in the empty caverns of his soul.

"How could this happen? How did this happen to me?" The questions raced through his head. "How could my life, which was pretty good, become such a mess in an instant?"
The questions were tormenting. There were no answers. All Sam knew was that his wife had left him for another man. His life seemed so empty, so meaningless.

The names and details may vary. But the same story repeats itself in real life over and over again. In many ways the death of a spouse is easier than a broken marriage. When a spouse chooses to leave, the grief is multiplied because the open wound of separation is salted with the pain of being rejected.

The best way to avoid the pain and heartache of a broken marriage is to establish the marriage on a firm foundation from the beginning. For many, the seeds of a broken marriage were sown during the dating process.

Where Did You Get Your Ideas about Dating?

If you are old enough to read this book then you likely have some notion about what dating is and what marriage is like. But, where did these ideas come from and are they right? Someone's view of marriage (and dating) are often learned from culture, civil law, observation, family and personal experience. The problem is that preconceived ideas about marriage can hinder understanding the true nature of marriage.

To gain an accurate understanding of marriage may require setting aside previously held ideas. A correct understanding of marriage originates from God who created marriage. In many instances, marriages are based on the crumbling foundation of the world's view of marriage (and dating) rather than being based on what God has revealed in the Bible. Entering marriage with a wrong understanding of what it is often contributes to its future failure.

Admittedly, it is never easy to lay aside what we hold to be true in order to learn what is actually true. However, humbly accepting what God says about marriage may make the difference between marital bliss, or hell on earth in your marriage experience.

Purposeful effort is needed to objectively define marriage as God does without being adversely influenced by outside sources.

To attain to a biblical understanding of marriage requires that the question be asked, "What does God say about marriage?"

The question is not "What do I think?" The issue is not "What does the government say is right or legal?" Marriage is not defined by answering the questions "What did my parents do?" or, "What does everyone else do?" To understand marriage one must ask the question, "What does God say?"

Regardless of the difficulty, we need to respect God as the creator of marriage and seek to know His mind on this issue. An accurate understanding of marriage will consist of agreement with God who has created marriage. He has told us about marriage in His Word, the Bible. We must be willing to listen.

It is not enough just to hear what God has said. We must be ready and willing to change the way we think to match what He thinks. The biblical term for this type of change in thinking is repentance. In a positive sense, we need to allow God to reprogram our thinking. We need to allow God to cleanse our minds and to replace our thoughts with His thoughts. This cleansing and replacing process results in Christian growth and maturity.[3] After all, faith is knowing what God says and agreeing with it.

Before considering what the Bible says about marriage it will be helpful to spend a little time reflecting on what we already think about marriage. Often we have opinions but do not even realize what they are until we are forced to express them.

By answering the following questions two things will be accomplished. First you will have to identify and state what you already think about marriage. Second, you will be ready to compare what you already believe with what God says. This prepares us to change our thinking as needed. Write out your answers to the following marriage related questions. Use your own words and answer each question to the best of your ability.

1. I would define marriage as...

2. I think that two people should get married when . . .

3. Of marriages today, approximately _____% end in divorce.

4. Valid reasons for getting a divorce include . . .

5. I would define love as . . .

6. I think the most important ingredients for having a "successful marriage" are . . .

If you did not complete any of the above questions it is strongly recommended that you do so before continuing. Your understanding of marriage will be clearer in your own mind if you do. Stating in advance what we think provides a way of keeping us honest. This is important. When we state what we believe, and are then confronted with a different answer from the Bible, we are compelled to make a decision. Am I right, or is God right? For if, after considering what the Bible says, we reach the same conclusion as our previously held position, we may need to question our attitude toward God and His authority. Perhaps the outcome of our inquiry was influenced by preconceived ideas more than by God's Word. Perhaps not. In either case answering the questions in advance provides an opportunity to evaluate whether we are allowing the Bible to speak for itself. Or, are we just reading our ideas into the Bible?[4]

---

3   Romans 12:1-2

4   2 Timothy 3:16 says the Word of God is profitable for instruction (providing information and facts) for reproof (showing where we are wrong) for correction (setting us straight) for training in righteousness (enabling us to do what is right). This process occurs as we allow the Spirit of God to apply the Word of God to our lives.

Although all the above questions are not specifically answered in this chapter, they will help you to begin to think consciously about marriage. Many of the associated issues will be discussed in the pages to follow.

You May Be a Statistic

Although Sam's story was fabricated, it is typical of the experiences of many people. Statistically, you are just as likely to be a Sam as not. Although there are many factors leading someone to Sam's position, one major contributor is getting married without understanding marriage according to God. Before considering what God has specifically stated, it will be helpful to consider marriage generally as it exists in the world.

Marriage Is Everywhere

Marriage is a worldwide norm. Generally speaking, marriage exists among all cultures and societies with slight variations in how marriage is viewed and practiced. Although there are some differences in the details, both civilized and uncivilized societies throughout the world practice marriage as a mutually exclusive intimate covenant relationship.

Along with the public recognition of the unique and exclusive relationship of marriage, boundaries of conduct are established. When these recognized boundaries are crossed it is considered wrong. Admittedly, these boundaries change with time and reflect the changing mind set of the populace. Yet marriage still remains part of the normal and common human experience.

In addition to the universal existence of marriage across all cultures, there is also an inherent individual awareness of marriage being right and normal and divorce being a painful tragedy. Each person intuitively knows that the relationship between a man and woman is exclusive and special. Spouses are universally and intuitively protective, defensive, and jealous for their partner. This is true of the first infatuation as a youngster and throughout adulthood. A person with a definite fondness for another tends to want to preserve that one exclusively for himself. Universally, the existence of marriage and the general boundaries of marriage seem to arise from within the human soul, even though marriage may be distorted in many cultures.

Although these observation are significant, a biblical understanding of marriage is not reached by observing how things are in the world. Although marriage is common, there are significant cultural variations in how marriage is viewed and practiced. This is increasingly true in Western culture where homosexual "marriages" are now gaining acceptance. It is noteworthy though, that all people have an inclination toward marriage somewhat consistent with what the Bible teaches about the creation of mankind.

13

Marriage Was Instituted by God

Faith in God acknowledges that God created mankind in His image and instituted marriage for our good. So to find marriage as a common institution within all cultures is no surprise. However, marriage as instituted by God is more definitive than the breadth of what is practiced in the world. Much of what is common in the world within marriages is contrary to what God instituted.

God's Prescription for Marriage

The Genesis 1 account of creation is a big picture overview of God's creative work and decrees. Genesis 2 offers a close up view of some portions of that same creation week.[5] The first account reveals that mankind is created in the image of God.[6] Significantly, God created mankind in His image as male and female. It may be that the image of God is jointly possessed by the man and woman in a way which may not be true of either one individually.[7] Such a conclusion is supported by the use of the singular and plural in referring to the creation of "man." God said, "Let us make man/mankind (singular) in Our image . . ." Then God blessed *them* and told *them* (plural) to rule over the earth. Thus mankind as a whole, including distinctions between the male and female gender, was created in the image of God.

Genesis 2:7-25 gives a more detailed look at a portion of the sixth day of creation that include what we know as marriage. The creation of the man (male) is described first and then the creation of the woman follows. Although at the end of the sixth day it is proclaimed that all God made was very good,[8] during that same sixth day of creation something was stated to be "not good." God said that it was "not good for the man to be alone."[9] It was "not good" because there was no helper suitable for the man. The man was not complete without his corresponding counterpart, the woman. It was the creation of the woman that changed the "not good" in the midst of the sixth day of creation to "very good"

---

5   This view of the two creation accounts is strongly supported by Jesus when He quotes from both accounts in response to a question about marriage. See Matthew 19:4-5

6   Genesis 1:26-28 Then God said, "Let Us make man in Our image, according to Our likeness; and let them rule over the fish of the sea and over the birds of the sky and over the cattle and over all the earth, and over every creeping thing that creeps on the earth." And God created man in His own image, in the image of God He created him; male and female He created them. And God blessed them; and God said to them, "Be fruitful and multiply, and fill the earth, and subdue it; and rule over the fish of the sea and over the birds of the sky, and over every living thing that moves on the earth."

7   Singleness, along with its role in the life of a Christian, will be discussed in another chapter.

8   Genesis 1:31

9   Genesis 2:18 Then the LORD God said, "It is not good for the man to be alone; I will make him a helper suitable for him.

at the end of the sixth day. It took both the man and the woman to make it "very good" and the relationship between the man and woman in marriage is included.[10]

Not only was God pleased with His creation of the man and woman, but He also had something instructive to say about the future relationship between a man and a woman. Genesis 2:24 says "For this cause a man shall leave his father and his mother, and shall cleave to his wife; and they shall become one flesh." Adam and Eve were the first couple and it is easily seen that the instructions given were about future couples as well.

In this statement God established the standard for men and women in what is called marriage. The mention of "father and mother" reveals that the statement is not limited to the first man and woman. The first man and woman did not have a mother and father. The intent of God's statements permanently applied to their descendants.[11]

Significantly, the establishment of marriage included a helper suitable to and corresponding to the male and the command to be fruitful and multiply.[12] Marriage, as intended by God, was not just about sex or companionship, it included procreation. Any notion of same sex marriage is completely absent.

At creation God made a three part proclamation about marriage. Marriage includes three components that happen simultaneously: leaving, cleaving and uniting. The first two actions, leaving and cleaving, are to be taken by the man. A marriage impacts relationships between the man and the woman as well as their individual families. Specifically, the man leaves his previous family unit upon being joined to his wife, forming a new and separate family unit. Marriage requires the man's "leaving" in order for him to be wholly devoted to his wife, thereby "cleaving." According to the New Testament this devotion is expressed in Christ-like love and provides his wife with an unquestionable security.[13]

A husband's lingering devotion and attachment to parents is often a cause of marital strife. To the husband, severing the ties with father and mother may seem insignificant. Yet for the wife, the man's willingness to leave his father and mother is essential to provide assurance that she is first and foremost in his life from the wedding day forward.[14]

---

10 This interdependence is seen in the New Testament as well. (I Corinthians 11:11 However, in the Lord, neither is woman independent of man, nor is man independent of woman.)

11 Jesus makes reference to both Genesis 1:27 and 2:24 in the discussion about divorce recorded in Matthew 19:1-12. In doing so He supports that both are accounts of the same creation. He also endorses marriage as the human norm.

12 Genesis 2:18-20 and 1:27-28

13 See Ephesians 5:25-33 These aspects will be addressed more fully in later chapters.

14 This also will be discussed in more detail in the chapters on the roles of husbands and wives. Regardless

God explicitly states that the man must leave his father and mother. Individual attention is called to each parent. Fathers and mothers play unique roles in the lives of their children. The man is required to sever himself from both. Such cutting of ties makes the man an independent agent who will lead his own family.

Of course, this severing is not an abandoning of one's parents. God expects that children will honor their father and mother all of their life. Marriage does not eliminate the command to honor father and mother. The "leaving" is establishing new priorities regarding the man's relationships with his parents and his wife. After marriage, the wife and her concerns are more important to him than those of his parents. It is important that the man clearly demonstrate to his wife in practical ways that she is number one to him. Leaving is setting priorities of relationships regardless of whether or not there is physical distance. However, many find that putting some physical distance between households makes the change in priorities both easier to implement and more obvious for parents and children alike.

Failure of the man to leave his parents is the source of much strife in marriages, as is evident in the abundance of in-law jokes. Most jokes target the husband and his mother-in-law. There are surprisingly few jokes about the wife and her mother-in-law probably because this is more often where the real tension occurs.

On the other hand, husbands who do "leave" parents are frequently misunderstood by their parents. For a harmonious marriage it is important that all parties understand that a man's wife replaces his parents in terms of loyalty and first consideration. The husband clearly leaving his parents is what will enable his wife to embrace her husband's parents without feeling threatened by them. If the man gives preference to his parents over his wife, the parents will threaten the wife's security. Good relationships between the young couple and the parents depend on their mutual devotion to one another and the relative distancing of themselves from their previous family roles and relationships.

God also says that the man shall "cleave to his wife." The word "cleave" means to cling or to adhere. When used in a figurative sense as it is here, the word means to "catch by pursuit." Cleaving describes the devotion that the Israelites were to have toward God. They were to cling to God.[15] The term also describes the leprosy which was to cling to the body of Elisha's servant.[16] Though perhaps not too romantic, the picture vivid. The husband is to cling to his wife like leprosy clings

---

of physical proximity, the husband who puts his relationship with parents above his relationship with his wife will create much marital friction and conflict.

15 Deuteronomy 10:20 You shall fear the LORD your God; you shall serve Him and cling to Him, and you shall swear by His name.

16 2 King 5:27 Therefore, the leprosy of Naaman shall cleave to you and to your descendants forever." So he went out from his presence a leper {as white} as snow.

to the body of the leper. Cleaving is an inseparable adherence, as if super glue had bonded the skin of each to the other.[17]

Notably, there is no mention of the bride leaving or cleaving. It is the man's responsibility to make the break and to devote himself to his wife. The wife's obligations to her husband are made clear in other Scripture passages. Perhaps the wife's continued relationship with her parents does not adversely impact the marriage relationship since the man does not need to have the same sense of security that the wife does. The first two components of marriage are leaving and cleaving, both actions taken by the man.

The third component of marriage is that ." . . they shall become one flesh." In God's view of marriage, one plus one equals one. The union of a man and woman in marriage results in a bonding of the two in a way that is beyond human explanation. The two are no longer two, but one. In some ways they are two, for they can travel in two different directions. In other ways they are one. This is a mystery but no less a fact which God has revealed.[18]

The verb translated "become," or "be," emphasizes the end result of being one, rather than the progressing toward becoming one. Although to "be one," they must at some time "become one." While it does not seem necessary to determine exactly when and how the oneness occurs, there is some reason to believe it is associated with the consummation of the marriage through the physical relationship.[19]

The mystery of the union in marriage is likely related to mankind being created in the image of God.

> Then God said, "Let *Us* make man in *Our* image, according to *Our* likeness; and let *them* rule over . . . the earth." God created man in *His* own image, in the image of God He created *him*; *male* and *female* He created *them*. Genesis 1:26 -27 (emphasis added)

In these words there is an interchangeable use of plural and singular nouns and pronouns referring to God and to mankind. As the triune God is one and yet Father, Son and Holy Spirit, so was man/mankind created male and female yet is one. In the image of God He . . . created them. As the Trinity is beyond complete comprehension and explanation so is the "one flesh" union between a man and a woman in marriage. Although it is inexplicable, and must be accepted by faith, it is the way marriage is.

---

17   It is impossible for a man to "cleave" to his wife and divorce her. See Matthew 19:1-6

18   See Ephesians 5:25-33

19   The concept of one flesh is associated with sexual intercourse in some texts rather than a recognized marriage ceremony. For example, 1 Corinthians 6:16 states "Or do you not know that the one who joins himself to a harlot is one body {with her}? For He says, "The two will become one flesh."

Additionally, a correlation is made in some of the letters to the churches in the New Testament regarding the spiritual relationship between Christ and the church. The relationship between a husband and wife is like the relationship between Jesus and His church.[20]

In salvation there is a similar union between Christ and the one who is saved. This too is beyond comprehension. Just because something is not fully explained does not mean it is false. In marriage, the man and woman become one. Significantly, Jesus refers to this truth in His response to a question about divorce. ("So they are no longer two, but one flesh. What therefore God has joined together, let no man separate." Matthew 19:6)[21]

Marriage was God's plan, God's design and God's idea. Not man's.

- God made men to be men and women to be women.

- God joins together the man and woman in marriage.

- God commands the man to cleave to his wife.

God is the creator of marriage as surely as He is the creator of anything. Marriage is a human relationship with divine origin. Marriage is God's idea. Marriage is also God's ideal, and "He saw it was very good."

God's role in establishing marriage is the correct starting point for any meaningful and objective discussion about marriage (and dating). Omitting God's revelation and instruction from the discussion results in exactly the type of confusion and chaos that exists in many societies today. Rejection of what God says about marriage is also the cause of much heartache and grief that many people experience in marriage.

Problems in marriages exist because, apart from Adam and Eve, marriage involves human decisions. The act of leaving one's parents and cleaving to a spouse is based on a decision to do so. Human choices become terms of a covenant which is an agreement between two people before God. The terms of the marriage covenant are often expressed in the wedding vows.

God is a third party in the marriage covenant. When vows are made to one's spouse they are made before God and also to God. From the beginning of time, God has been involved. Marriage is more than a piece of paper, a legal status and some shared property. Marriage is the divine uniting of two people resulting in the retention of their individuality and the union of two persons to form one. Thus

---

20 Ephesians 5:25-33

21 A subsequent chapter will discuss at length the biblical teachings and the common positions held by churches regarding divorce and remarriage.

Jesus said, ." . . what God has joined together, let no man separate." (Matthew 19:6)

From these Bible texts a preliminary definition of marriage can be derived:

Marriage is a lifelong, divinely established relationship of commitment between a man and a woman resulting in the two becoming one.

Lesser views of marriage are often the cause for marriage failures. When marriage is embraced as being established by God it greatly increases the likelihood that it will endure and be successful.

To avoid the "hell on earth" often associated with failed marriages, the gravity of the relationship God created must be understood. God is involved in every marriage. Marriage is two becoming one for life.

Understanding marriage as God intended is foundational and essential to having an enduring, happy and successful marriage. So how does dating relate to marriage? Most would agree that dating precedes and often leads to marriage. What is God's perspective on dating and how should Christians view dating?

Chapter 2
Assumptions and Dating

A father was overheard lamenting to his pastor,

"The other day, Maggie, our oldest daughter asked me if she could begin dating. She is only 15. Most of her friends at school and church are starting to date. She wants to be allowed to date too. She is a good girl and wants to follow God. When I told her I don't think it is a good idea for to start dating, she challenged me, "Why not?!." When I told her I did not think God wanted her to date so young, she asked me, "Dad, can you show me from the Bible why 15 is too young to begin dating?" I know I am right. I have tried to find Bible verses to answer her question but I am coming up empty. Can you help me?"

If you were that pastor, how would you respond? What would be the biblical basis for your response? What verses would you offer?

Most parents and pastors have a "position" on dating. However, when it comes to demonstrating that their position is based on the Bible they often gasp and flail like a fish out of water. (Children develop opinions about dating and most also would have trouble supporting their position from Scripture.) Although the father's answer could legitimately be "because I am the Dad," it is much better to understand the issues clearly and to be able to apply biblical principles directly to life issues.

Seriously Thinking About Dating

The intent of this chapter is largely to stimulate thought. Some who read this book may be a bit resistant to having someone tell them what to do. So, instead of giving hard and fast rules for dating, there will be encouragement to think for yourself, and to think honestly. Instead of being told what to think, you will be asked ponder a variety of subjects and issues related to dating.

As dating is discussed, the traditional and cultural views will be challenged. Widely held assumptions will be confronted and put to the test. Biblical texts will be identified and related principles will be derived.

When our beliefs are challenged, it is natural for us to feel threatened - to resist and to reject what is being suggested. However, God frequently challenges us as a way of transforming our hearts. A humble person in submission to Christ will carefully consider what God has to say. The result will be a life pleasing to God and pleasant experiences for the one who follows God.

There are four results that can be expected when God's Word is seriously considered. God, through His Word <u>instructs</u> (communicates facts), <u>reproves</u> (shows where we are wrong), <u>corrects</u> (shows us what is right), and finally <u>trains</u> us that we might be able to do what we should.[22]

Throughout this book an effort has been made to clearly separate biblical teaching from the author's suggestions. Suggestions are offered throughout the chapter in attempt to accomplish two purposes:

1. to promote thoughtful evaluation of actions, practices and their outcomes, and

2. to offer some practical ways to implement the biblical principles.

Where the author is offering suggestions for implementation they will be identified with the word "THOUGHT:" You can take all, part or none of these suggestions and perhaps still be pleasing to God. However, you will not please God if you reject any clear biblical instruction or principle. When God's instructions are rejected the consequences are frequently unpleasant and sometimes experienced as hell on earth.

How One Learns About Dating

A six year old boy attended his first wedding. Upon returning home he peered across the fence into the neighbor's yard where little girl was playing. He called out, "Hey! Do you want to get married?"

What each person believes about dating has been learned. A 16 year old probably has an opinion about dating but a 6 year old may not. A two year old child has no idea what dating is. So it is clear that each person's perspective on dating is something they have learned.

Like many things in life, dating is usually learned through observation and by example. Unfortunately, or perhaps in many instances fortunately, children do not have the opportunity to observe their parents dating. The "ins and outs" of the dating process are learned from peers, siblings and the media. Dating, like many things in life, is usually something that is "caught" more than it is "taught."

Rarely are children given specific instructions about dating. Rarer still is a young person whose view of dating is clearly based on God's Word. More often than not, churches and parents alike fail to address dating directly apart from scattering

---

22 2 Timothy 3:16-17 and Romans 12:1-2 make it clear that the four-fold work of the Word of God is to challenge and change how we think to how God thinks, that we might be perfect and complete.

a few warnings and taboos. The sad and sometimes tragic result is that most young people approach the dating process in a haphazard, and frequently unbiblical fashion. This is true of both the churched and unchurched, of believers and unbelievers.

In most societies, the form dating takes is traditionally accepted and culturally determined. As such, the unexpressed but prevailing thinking seems to be "My parents dated; my peers date; my siblings date: dating is normal; therefore, I will date. Someday I may marry, but for now I will just date until that happens or until I make up my mind." It is not unusual, in Western cultures at least, to find children of elementary age engaging in activities and behaviors associated with "dating." Schools host proms, and it is assumed that dating is normal and good without a second thought.

The challenge for the Christian is to evaluate the traditional and cultural norms in the light of biblical teaching. Christians should look to the teaching of Scripture and be motivated by a desire to please God in everything, including dating. Much of what is taken for granted about dating is planted in one's mind at an early age. This prior programming may hinder clearly seeing God's will and understanding what pleases Him. To know the mind of God requires a willingness to lay aside preconceived ideas and to do what God says.

Wisdom in Dating

The Bible repeatedly makes it very clear that reverence for God is the beginning of knowledge and wisdom.[23] Arriving at a conclusion about dating that pleases God will depend on having a humble spirit of submission before Him. Humility means that you understand that God, first as the Creator, and also as Savior and Lord, has the indisputable right to dictate what your life should include and what should be excluded. It would be wise and appropriate to pause now and ask God to give you a humble spirit and the wisdom about dating that only He can give.

Assessing What You Currently Believe: A Personal Inventory

Questions are asked to help you begin to think with discernment about dating. Respond carefully to the following questions to the best of your ability. Be honest with yourself. Think carefully about giving your answers before writing them down on a separate paper. For the true or false questions, please explain your answers.

1. List all of the things that the Bible says about dating.

2. In your own words you would define a date as . . .

3. List all of the things that happen on dates.

4. The purpose of a date is . . .

---

23 Proverbs 1:7 & 9:10, for example

5. T or F - Dating is a good way to really get to know someone.

6. T or F - How people get along on dates is a good indication of how they will get along once they are married.

7. T or F - Sexual activity during dating is OK as long as you do not go "all the way."

8. T or F - Men and women generally understand and appreciate how the other will respond in a dating relationship.

9. T or F - Parents are a good sounding board when considering whether or not to date someone.

10. T or F - You should only date someone you consider to be an eligible marriage partner.

11. T or F - People on dates put on appearances to make an impression.

12. T or F - God approves of dating.

13. T or F - You can expect the behavior of the person you marry to be different than it was when you were dating.

The value you gain from the discussion that follows will increase in proportion to the thought and honesty demonstrated in answering the above questions. Many of the issues raised by these questions will be discussed and evaluated in the pages to follow.

Preaching and Practicing (An author's confession)

At the time of writing the second edition of this book, I am over fifty-five years old. I have been happily married to only one woman for thirty four years, and I have seven beautiful children. I readily acknowledge that what is preached in this chapter is not what I practiced before marriage when I was dating. However, what is preached is what I would practice if I had it to do again.

There are several reasons for the differences between what I did and what I should have done. I was not walking in obedience to the Lord when I was dating nor when we married. I was not seeking to please the Lord but primarily myself. By God's grace, shortly after marriage, I began walking with the Lord and seeking to please Him. In the few months after my wedding day until the Lord inclined my heart toward Him, my marriage was a great challenge. I frequently wondered how long my marriage would last.

My experience of living in disobedience followed by walking with the Lord has validated what the Lord has said in His Word about marriage. That which follows is not based on personal experience but rather based upon the revealed will of God in His Word. Many of the thoughts and questions are raised to highlight the faulty thinking of those of us who don't know, or choose to ignore what God has said.

A Dating Disaster

A lump hung in Joanne's throat. Tears pressed like water piled behind a high bulging dam upon her bright blue eyes. A load of gravel had been dumped in her knotted stomach. The 17 year old daughter of a successful pastor stared blankly into the brook as water danced over the smooth rocks meandering into the forest. The late summer breeze tickled the leaves whispering a message of tranquility. All around her was calm and peace. Yet deep inside an emotional storm was relentlessly ripping strips of flesh from Joanne's heart.

She had not wanted it to happen. She had not planned for it to happen. But it had happened. Her soul was tormented by the question, "Why did this happen?" Her reason protested, "This is not the way things are supposed to be!" The events, like scenes from a scary movie looping in nightmares replayed over and over. Her will kept pushing the thoughts away. She could not turn them off.

Alternately her thoughts turned to what others would say if they knew. In sequence she pictured the responses of people when they learned what had happened: her mom, the belligerent deacon, the youth leader, her friends. Her mind flashed randomly from scene to scene – and she sat still – petrified by it all. These things were not supposed to happen, especially to the daughter of the pastor.

Although she tried to resist thinking of her father, he constantly climbed to center stage in her mind. What would all this mean for him? Would her father resign? He had always stated matter-of-fact that his family was the basis for his ministry. Now, would his ministry be over because of something that happened, "innocently enough"? But it shouldn't have happened.

A few months earlier, Charles and his family began attending church. They had moved from another town, and Charles was understandably the chatter of all the young ladies. He was strong, tall and handsome. But beyond that, he was nice on the inside and obviously polite and courteous to people of all ages. He carried his Bible everywhere and always spoke of the Lord. All the adults seemed to like Charles. Frequently Joanne would hear older folks comment about his zeal and commitment to God.

Joanne had also noticed Charles right away like the rest. To her pleasure, and surprise, before long he seemed to have noticed her too. After church one Sunday evening, he asked if he could give her a ride home. After obtaining permission from her parents, she was thrilled to be chauffeured home by the popular, polite and attractive young man. In the days to follow Joanne found numerous opportunities to be with Charles.

They greatly enjoyed being together. He was fun. He was funny. Cute too. They laughed and joked. Chills ran up Joanne's spine when one evening after youth group Charles gently held her hand. As the days passed they frequently held hands and it seemed wonderful. Soon they shared a hug and then a shy kiss. "This must be like heaven," Joanne would say to herself.

But now she felt terrible. Heaven's streets of gold had been dashed into a million pieces. Guilt flooded her soul. If they only had stayed with the youth group. If they only had stayed where there were people. If only she had . . . or if only he had . . . stopped.

It started innocently enough. A desire to be together away from the noise. A drive to a secluded place. A smile. First a kiss and then another. The passion grew until Charles was touching her places where she knew he shouldn't. Yet she did not want to say "No." Actually, apart from the guilt which she felt deep inside, it was increasingly exciting and pleasurable.

Finally the sense of wrong became overwhelming. Joanne struggled free and lunged from the car. "Stop! We can't!" she exclaimed in fear and confusion. After an eternal moment of silence she quietly said, "Will you please take me back? Now?" Charles starting the car, whimpered, "I'm sorry."

They returned without speaking a word and joined the group with barely a notice. Being unable to look at each other the rest of the evening made everything miserable. The earlier events so flooded Joanne's mind that no other thought could enter. Finally, after an eternity had passed, it was time to go home.

Joanne asked a girl-friend for a ride home. So many questions filled her mind. How could such a thing happen when she had done everything right? She did not date an unbeliever. She did not go with a boy of whom her parents disapproved. They were both devoted Christians. What went wrong?

The names, events and characters in the above story are fictitious. Yet versions of the same story are repeated in real life with great frequency. Often the results are more life changing and significant than those which Joanne experienced. Frequently neither person has what it takes to stop what their actions have set into motion.

What Went Wrong?

Underlying Joanne's experience were unquestioned assumptions about dating. The assumptions seem fairly harmless - the way things are done is the way they should be done, and therefore it is the right way to do them. It is assumed that if this is what other "good Christian people" do, or what everyone else does, then this must be the way it should be done. The problem is that the assumptions are embraced without asking what God says or considering what God wants when it comes to dating.

Most people do not even think to ask, "What does God say about dating?" Many well-meaning Christian people just assume that dating is acceptable to God. Likewise, they assume that dating is to be conducted as others have done it, as it "has always been done." After all, nowhere in the Bible does one find the eleventh commandment recorded, "Thou shall not date." Of course, some questions are asked. Youth leaders, pastors and parents often give instructions and impose boundaries on dating.

Yet, there is a need to ask more basic and foundational questions. There is a need to ask more questions. These questions need to be addressed to God and answered by the Holy Spirit through God's Word. So . . .

What Does God Say About Dating?

Go ahead. Get out the Bible and look up "dating" or "date." Guess what? Strike one. Now try to find "courting" and other associated words. (Some suggest dating is unbiblical but courting is the right way.) Strike two. Okay then. Try "boyfriend" or "girlfriend." Strike three. The Bible does not use these words. Neither does the Bible give specific instructions about either dating or courtship.

There should be no doubt that God is concerned about dating. The Bible has lots to say about issues associated with dating. But the Bible does not provide direct teaching. Instead, a biblical understanding of dating comes from knowing its purpose and gaining God's perspective.

A Fun Little Exercise

Test your pastor, your youth pastor or even your parents. Certainly any of them would jump at the chance to teach you about dating God's way. Right? Just tell them that you are interested in finding out what the Bible has to say about dating and watch their eyes light up. (Have a phone ready because you may need to call 9-1-1 for medical assistance if they have a heart attack.) Then as they turn to passages simply ask, "now is this talking about dating or is it talking about something else, like marriage, or sexual immorality, or . . . ?"

What about 1 Corinthians 15:33? ."..Bad company corrupts good morals." This is a dating verse, right? Wrong! This verse is talking about the negative influence of those who have an incorrect view of the resurrection. This text is not about friends or dating but rather about fellowship in the church with people who believe false doctrine.[24]

Then what about 2 Corinthians 6:14 which says "Do not be unequally yoked?" This is a verse about dating, isn't it? No. In what sense is dating being "bound?" Most would agree that dating is more like shopping than it is like entering into a binding agreement or relationship. Of course dating frequently leads to being bound. Thus, one should keep this passage in mind. Still, it is not speaking directly to dating. However there may be principles that apply to dating.

Those who understand the Bible will be quick to point out that dating is not directly addressed by God in His Word. Indeed, there are stories about courtship and marriage, both good and bad. But there are no direct or definitive statements on "how to date," "who to date," "when to date," "why to date" or "where to date."

As sin and immorality are increasingly tolerated in our society, Christians should be increasingly alarmed about many issues, including "dating." Some, out of such concern, have written books promoting "courtship" rather than "dating" as God's way for Christian people. The problem is that the Bible does not address courtship any more directly than it addresses dating. So even if in some people's mind courtship seems safer and better than dating, Scripture does not advocate either one.

One's understanding of dating must be derived from Scriptural principles of marriage, relationships and moral conduct to be truly godly and biblically based. The narrative accounts of courting and marriage in the Bible just tell how things were done, not how they should be done.

Admittedly, some narratives in the Bible more clearly resemble what would be called courtship than they do modern dating. Other narratives include incest, adultery, polygamy, prearranged marriage, secretly coming to the feet of a sleeping man, taking a widow to be a second wife within a week of her husband's death, etc. Just because the Bible describes something in a narrative does not mean it provides a pattern to be followed.

---

24 See the author's book, *"Good Sermon, Brother!"* for a thorough, but concise, discussion of principles of Bible interpretation.

Christian behavior and standards must be based on direct teaching and principles rather than following examples in a narrative. Narratives may contain either good or bad examples. Without God's commentary on the narrative or other direct biblical teaching on a subject, it is an error to hold a particular historical account as the correct and God-endorsed pattern.

Chapter 3
Defining Dating

For simplicity sake, the generic term "dating" will be used in this book even though some may prefer the term "courting." The actual term used is irrelevant. The issue, regardless of what the process is called, is whether or not the attitudes and behavior in dating are pleasing to God or not. Carefully following God's principles in order to be pleasing to God is what is needful regardless of what title the process is given, whether courtship or dating.

Although there is a lack of direct teaching in the Bible about dating, there are fortunately many principles that explain what God expects of His children in these matters. There are also scriptural principles that apply directly and indirectly to dating. First the principles that apply to dating need to be identified and then need to be clearly understood.

<u>Questions of Inquiry</u>

Again, answer some questions to help identify the issues associated with dating and to begin considering what biblical principles may apply. As a starting point consider these questions:

- What is a date?
- What does the dating process include?
- When does dating start?
- What are the steps within dating?
- What is the finish of dating?
- What is the purpose of dating?
- What is the goal of dating?

These questions help bring light to the various aspects of dating that might otherwise be left in obscurity. Asking these questions will get to the heart of dating and will assist in determining how God views the dating process. Identifying the parts, activities, motives and goals in dating will enable comparison with what God says are appropriate activities, motives and goals in all areas of life.

<u>Defining a Date</u>

For the sake of clarity and discussion it is necessary to define the term "date." For the purpose of this discussion there are many forms of dates, appointments and encounters which fall outside the scope of dating. With this in mind, and for the sake of a common reference point, the following non-technical definition of a date is offered:

> A date is a predetermined <u>time</u> during which two people of the <u>opposite sex</u> spend time together, <u>focused</u> on each other, even though they may be in the presence of other people.

This is a general and inclusive definition but it serves well as a starting point to focus attention where needed. Excluded from the definition is going out with "the girls" or "the guys." Chance meetings are not dates but may become a date when time and attention are devoted to one another.[25] Double dating and group dating may fall inside or outside the definition depending on the purpose and focus of the arrangement. Excluded also are appointments, meetings, etc, which are for business or other purposes.

<u>Why Date?</u>

Why date? This is perhaps one of the most important questions young people should honestly ask. Carefully answering this question is essential to be pleasing to God. How this question is answered separates the world's dating from Christian dating. Additionally, how this question is answered is the heart of why some Christians embrace courtship rather than dating.

Most people seem to think that dating "just happens" without intentional direction or focus. The idea is that when young people get to a certain age, it is natural for them to date - to spend time alone with a person of the opposite sex. Dating is seen as perhaps an extension of a friendship and as a social interaction that is a loose and casual precursor to an eventual marriage relationship.

To view dating in this way is to thoughtlessly "go with the flow" of our obviously ungodly society. Individuals involved in dating usually have an intent and motives, just like all of life's other activities. Everything a person does has a motive, even if it is not verbalized or consciously known. As in most things, the motive for a person dating is usually left unexpressed. Sometimes the intent of the date is even purposefully and deceitfully hidden. Some people may hide their motives for a date because they actually know that they would be unacceptable.

Motives for dates vary widely, and wildly. Dating motives may include dispelling loneliness, desiring a friend, seeking affirmation, getting a free dinner, sexual gratification and everything in between. If a boy on a date is seeking sexual gratification and the girl is just wanting casual conversation and a meal, it is obvious that one or both will be disappointed.

---

25 Two people who have a chance meeting in a group can focus on one another to the extent that they are oblivious to the other people around.

THOUGHT: An interesting exercise would be to write down and discuss the purpose for each date prior to it occurring. If the goal is to please God first, then motives in dating should be evaluated to make sure the date will please Him. Warning! Evaluating motives in advance will probably result in fewer dates. But, the more important question is "Do you really want to date with motives that are not pleasing to God?"

Beyond the motive in dating one needs to consider the purpose, function, and goal of dating. What is a date, or a series of dates supposed to accomplish? In order to evaluate dating practices, or a specific date, the function and purpose of dating needs to be determined. On a practical level, the purpose of a date may be identified by simply asking, "What happens on a date?" What actually happens on dates reveals the underlying purposes of dating.

Dates frequently include activities such as talking, eating, driving, recreational sports, observing how the other person responds in different situations, casual touching, kissing, intimate sexual activity, etc.[26] It can easily be seen that the purpose of dating is related to these activities in one way or another. By identifying the purpose and activities of dating, one has tangible data to evaluate dating using biblical standards. Another helpful question in assessing and defining dating is"who dates?."

Who Dates?

This may seem an odd question. Yet, the answer is actually quite enlightening. Most everyone knows who dates. Dating is practiced by a limited and select segment of the population.

- It is not normally little kids who go on dates.
- It is usually not people who are already married.
- The people who date are those who are "eligible."

In times past "eligible" clearly meant being a candidate for marriage. However, in today's society those who date are "eligible" for an unspecified relationship with another person. The relationship may, or may not include the potential for marriage. For most people, dating relationships include a progression from the casual to the intimate. Such progression, if not interrupted, eventually includes sexual intimacy.[27]

---

26 Indeed, those with worldly morals often view a date as the precursor event or stepping stone to an intimate sexual encounter. For Christians, such a purpose of dating would put dating clearly outside the expressed will of God. 1 Corinthians 6:9-10, 15-20 and 1 Thessalonians 4:1-8, for example, clearly prohibit sexual promiscuity of the Christian.

27 It is acknowledged that some people may "date," reach a plateau in the relationship and make no further progress toward intimate sexual activity. In general, this seems to be the exception rather than the rule.

The Bible is very clear that sexual intimacy is restricted only to marriage. Thus, the Christian who is dating needs to establish some limits in dating. Sex outside of marriage is a sin and is displeasing to God.

In today's world, however, dating is associated with relationships much less defined than in previous generations. Not too long ago a person was considered either married or single. Married people were not "eligible." Single people were "eligible." To be "eligible" meant that a person could be considered as a potential marriage partner, and therefore could be considered for pursuing through dating. Dating was previously considered as a precursor to marriage. Lines are less clear today and are becoming fuzzier all the time.

The confusion about dating in contemporary culture is compounded by the confusion about marriage and what constitutes an appropriate relationship. For example, in 2013, a popular social site provides many variations for a person's relational status including single, in a relationship, engaged, married, it's complicated, in an open relationship, separated, divorced, in a civil union, or in a domestic partnership. Increasingly, it is culturally acceptable for people, including those who claim to be Christians, to date, to have sex, to bear children and to live together. Marriage is considered to be unnecessary.

The Bible is very clear that sexual activity outside of marriage is a sin. It is either fornication or adultery.[28] It is equally clear that a person who is sinning sexually should not be considered to be saved.[29] Although cultures may fluctuate regarding what is acceptable behaviors, the Bible does not change. A biblical assessment of dating requires identifying the motives, activities and eventually the outcome of the relationship.[30]

Clarifying the Purpose of Dating

Ask yourself, "If I get married, will I continue to date other people?" The answer should be clearly "No!" for some very significant reasons. Once married, you will no longer date because your spouse would (hopefully) disapprove. The other reason why you will no longer date is because marriage has fulfilled the purposes of dating. Of course a married person may spend time with their spouse and call it a date. But "dating" someone other than your spouse is considered wrong by most people even in today's permissive and immoral society.

28 Fornication is a broad term referring to any sexual activity outside of marriage. Adultery is specifically having sex with someone other than your spouse.

29 1 Corinthians 6:9-11 Or do you not know that the unrighteous will not inherit the kingdom of God? Do not be deceived; neither fornicators, nor idolaters, nor adulterers, nor effeminate, nor homosexuals, nor thieves, nor the covetous, nor drunkards, nor revilers, nor swindlers, will inherit the kingdom of God. Such were some of you; but you were washed, but you were sanctified, but you were justified in the name of the Lord Jesus Christ and in the Spirit of our God. See also Galatians 5:19-21.

30 Remember, that the assumption of this book is that you are a committed Christian who is seeking to please God. To please God we must allow our natural thoughts to be replaced by God's thoughts.

THOUGHT: Imagine being married. What would your response be if your spouse went on a date for a late night dinner at a dimly lit restaurant with someone other than you? In most cases fur would fly and rightly so. Indeed, people divorce when their spouse begins dating someone else. Christian wives come weeping to their pastors if their husband takes another woman on a date. It seems safe to assert that "married people do not date" anyone but their spouse.

THOUGHT: Ask this: "If a single Christian young woman is committed to life-long celibate[31] service to the Lord, would you expect her to date?" If she were to date, what would the purpose be? If her commitment to the Lord is sincere and firm, then where does that leave the man dating her? What are his assumptions about dating her? It seems doubtful a Christian person who is intending not to marry would be actively engaged in "dating."

If the above "thoughts" have a semblance of reason to them, then "dating," is only something practiced by those eligible to marry and, to one degree or another, by those anticipating marriage.[32] This should especially be the practice for Christians.

Equipped with God's instructions about sexual intimacy and understanding what happens on dates, some additional definitions can be offered.

The purpose of dating for the Christian could be stated:

Dating is a screening process to identify the one and only person you will marry and the only person with whom you will be sexually intimate for all of your life.[33]

Using this purpose of dating for the Christian, and the previous definition of a date, a Christian definition of dating would be as follows:

A date is a predetermined time during which two Christian people of the opposite sex spend time together, focused on each other, to assess whether or not they will get married.

---

31 To be celibate means to be sexually inactive. Singleness and celibacy will be discussed in a later chapter.

32 As culture moves more and more away from the God-intended monogamous marriage relationship, the purpose of dating also moves. The result is that, dating today for many is not in anticipation of marriage but in place of some aspects of marriage. Thus sexual encounters during "dates" are becoming more prevalent. This of course is outside of the expressed will of God.

33 Marriage is for life. The death of a spouse makes a Christian eligible for dating and marriage again. (see Romans 7:1-7 and 1 Corinthians 7:39)

It is not necessary to agree with these definition to benefit from the rest of this book. However, they provide a clear starting point to evaluate the dating process.

Although the Bible has little to say about "dating," it has much to say about relationships between individuals of the opposite sex. It also has much to say about the relationship between a husband and a wife. By viewing dating as anticipation of marriage the discussion of dating can be clearly and definitively viewed from a clear biblical vantage point.

Absent clear definitions of dates and dating leave the discussion clouded with vagueness. A clear definition of dating is required in order to assess it based on the Bible. Biblical evaluation of dating is essential to pleasing God.

Chapter 4
Principles for Dating

Dating: A Shadow of Deception

The typical date in American culture does not do a very good job of identifying whether or not someone will be a good husband or wife. It is common to hear a spouse complain, "He/She is not the person that I married." Usually they <u>are</u> exactly the person they married, but they just did not know who they were marrying.

Dating is in some ways like the distorted mirrors of a fun house. The typical date may even be counter-productive to developing a life-long relationship pleasing to God and pleasant to the marriage partners.

Often dating is limited to activities that are on the fringe of the ebb and flow of life. Dates include activities like a drive in the country, going to the movies, eating out, retreating to some secluded place or playing tennis together. These activities generally do not allow people to be observed and assessed in life's normal environment with its stresses, difficulties and struggles. Life's trials reveal a person's true character. Dating practices typically create artificial settings and situations where the real person remains intentionally hidden.

People put on their best clothes and their best face for a date. Significant effort is expended to impress the other person and to keep them from seeing who you truly are. The goal is to look your best and make the best impression. Extra care is taken to be on your best behavior. Conflict is avoided at all cost. Truthfulness is sacrificed to gain acceptance or to achieve the goals of the date. Dating in this way is deceptive at best. God expects His children to put off the lying and deceit.

"that, in reference to your former manner of life, you lay aside the old self, which is being corrupted in accordance with the lusts of deceit, and that you be renewed in the spirit of your mind, and put on the new self, which in {the likeness of} God has been created in righteousness and holiness of the truth. Therefore, laying aside falsehood, speak truth, each one {of you,} with his neighbor, for we are members of one another." Ephesians 4:22-25

One must ask if a typical date is in accordance with "the lusts of deceit" or if it exhibits the "holiness of the truth?"

Deceptive dating does not normally allow people to get to know the real person. The "dating person" is not the real person, but is a fake front that the real person puts on for the sake of gaining approval on the date. Getting along in marriage is vastly different than getting along with in a dating environment.

Thus it happens that two people who get along wonderfully while dating may not get along after they are married. Under the best conditions, it is a difficult task for two sinful human beings to live together in close quarters for an extended period of time. A typical dating relationship tends to hide, rather than reveal the true -nature and character of the potential marriage partner. Deceptive dating creates unrealistic expectations that cannot be sustained in marriage. The stage is thus set for disappointment and conflict.

> **Biblical Principle:** Dating should be conducted in a way that is truthful and transparent and not deceptive.

Dating Can Create Unhealthy Emotional Attachments

Generally speaking, it is not conducive to godliness for a man and a woman who are not married to one another to spend extended periods of time together.[34] Emotional attachments naturally form when one is on his best behavior treating someone of the opposite sex with kindness and consideration. Time spent together has an emotional impact on them even if others are present. The development of such bonds of attachments occur unbeknownst to them, even when they are unwanted and thought to be unsolicited.

John and Janet worked for the same company. Both were happily married with children. Both were committed to their spouses and children. Yet, a problem began to develop long before either of them realized there was even the potential for a problem. John and Janet were assigned to work together on a very critical project. It required their complete dedication, as well as much of their time and effort. Success meant much money for the company and likely a promotion for each of them. Both of them stepped up to the task with enthusiasm, thinking that a promotion and pay raises would be good for their families and their happiness in life.

At times, each of their spouses expressed resentment, and sometimes even anger, over their long hours spent away from home. The absence and long hours made life at home less pleasant and their spouses' displeasure put a strain on their marriages.

---

34   Those who suggest that dating is not a screening for marriage but is rather the expression of friendship to fill the need for companionship often fail to seriously grapple with this warning.

When at work John and Janet confided in one another regarding their struggles at home. They commiserated and consoled one another. At work there were the pleasantries, there was an effort to be nice. At home there seemed to be a lack of understanding on their spouses' part. The days passed. John and Janet each found they enjoyed being at work with their co-worker more than facing the tension at home. They became more and more fond of each other. They "grew apart" from their spouses as their emotional bond to each other grew. Soon they became sexually intimate.

Two marriages were damaged; two families were affected because two people allowed emotional bonds to develop. This story repeats itself wherever men and women spend time together and make an effort to be kind and nice to each other regardless of their marital status. Emotional bonds and affections grow between people who spend time together especially when they are treating one another well. The emotional bonds grow into physical attractions that, left unchecked, become the source of many broken homes. The nice woman at work becomes more attractive and desirable than the nagging wife at home.

Timothy was warned about these types of dangers and told to flee from them.

"Now flee from youthful lusts, and pursue righteousness, faith, love {and} peace, with those who call on the Lord from a pure heart." 2 Timothy 2:22

This type of affection develops between two previously happily married people with families. It is even more likely to happen between two unmarried highly hormonal young people who spend time together while making an effort to be nice. The emotional bonds that arise from being nice to one another is what people often call "falling in love." Typical dating is a process that encourages people to "fall in love" rather than to objectively assess the qualities and characteristics which one desires in a lifelong partner.

Emotions are very real. Emotions are powerful. Falling in love is an emotional response to another person and it is powerful. After a person has reached such an emotional state, it is quite painful, and often difficult to back out of the relationship. Thus people often marry based on an emotional relationship rather than on an actual assessment of the other person.[35]

Each person must be aware of dating's potential to build emotional bonds. They must guard their hearts by limiting their dating activities and keeping a clear focus on the purpose of dating.

---

35 For the Christian, one of the most important aspects of assessment is determining the spiritual state and maturity of the other person.

The natural tendency to develop emotional bonds is one of the reasons why young people need to be careful about becoming close friends with a person of the opposite sex. Friends spend time together. They enjoy each other's company. They open themselves up to their friends. They are nice to one another. Friends become emotionally attached. It is very difficult for a boy and girl to "just be friends." Generally, these friendships either grow in affection progressing toward intimacy, or they back off to become casual friends. It is rare that a close friendship between a boy and a girl remains close and stationary. Even if it is possible for one person to maintain an appropriate relationship, it often is not possible for the other. Thus, great care is needed to make sure the relationship remains appropriate and to ensure that the other person is not hurt.

Many Christians begin spending time with an unbeliever because they are fun or funny or provide for a good time. Next, they think, well, if it is okay to be friends, it is also okay to casually date. They start out with no intention to marry, but the dating relationship soon leads to affections of the heart. That affection then leads to considering marriage. At this point the believer has a clear choice to make: 1) either obey God and break off the relationship contrary to the inclinations of the heart, or 2) reject the command not to be unequally yoked[36], follow their emotions and marry. It is much better not to allow these emotional bonds to be established.

> **Biblical Principle**: Be on guard for emotional attachments that may lead away from what God wants.

Emotional attachment is often short lived. After marriage, the effort to be nice all the time gives way to the day to day grind. The emotional love fades with the jeans in the laundry. Such love tends to cool like dishwater left standing in the sink if the love is not regularly renewed. If the relationship is based solely on this emotional love, it will last only as long as the infatuation. In most cases, it does not take too long for the enchantment and excitement to pass. Successful and enduring marriages need a stronger foundation than the emotional love that typical dating relationships spawn.

Progress Toward Physical Problems

The stories about Joanne and Charles, as well as John and Janet, illustrate the progress of emotional attachment. Unchecked emotional momentum will snowball. The warm feelings soon graduate into gentle touches and soft caresses. This progression is remarkably predictable. Although the path may be taken unknowingly, and innocently enough, it does not happen by chance. Unless checked, the relationship between a man and a woman spontaneously grows in intimacy until it is completely fulfilled.

---

36 Although a Christian dating an unbeliever does not violate 2 Corinthians 6:14 which commands, Do not be bound together with unbelievers . . ., marrying an unbeliever clearly does violate the command.

Physical contact between a man and a woman affects men and women in profoundly different and dangerous ways. Usually, for the woman, the emotional aspect of the relationship is quite satisfying in and of itself. She is typically content just to be in his presence. To touch casually, hold hands or share a kiss or a hug is primarily a reinforcement of that emotional attachment for the woman. She experiences comfort, warmth and feelings of security as a result of the touching.

However, for the man, the physical aspect is something quite different. Emotional attraction is present but is often minimal compared to what the woman experiences. For the man, physical contact leads to desire for more physical contact, leading to the desire for even more physical contact. Physical contact with a girl is the match that lights his fire stacked high with dry kindling. For the man, the way dating is practiced often presents escalating temptations of which many girls or women are not aware. First there is the holding of hands, but this is not enough to satisfy for long. Then there is the kiss, but this is not enough to satisfy. Then the hug, but this is not enough to satisfy. Each step is pouring gasoline on the fire. Indeed, all these physical contacts are the addition of fuel to a fire that nothing short of sexual intercourse will adequately satisfy. This is all compounded by the raging river of hormones typically present in young men of dating age.

Such is the unchecked course that is set unwittingly in motion in many dating relationships. Those who are committed to the Lord often force themselves to put on the brakes at some point when the flames grow too high. The typical dating process builds fires requiring purposeful containment by both parties. While physical and sexual attraction will inevitably occur, it is much better not to build these unnecessary fires.

We are told to pray that God "lead us not into temptation"[37] but at the same time, by dating the way the world dates, people are unwittingly playing with the matches of temptation. The first chapter of James clearly identifies that our own desires are the source of our temptation. It says that God does not tempt us "but each one is tempted when he is carried away and enticed by his own lust. Then when lust has conceived, it gives birth to sin; and when sin is accomplished, it brings forth death." (James 1:14)

In the Sermon on the Mount, Jesus said that whatever causes a person to sin should be dealt with quickly and severely, that we might not sin.[38] Jesus was addressing adultery specifically and immorality in general. It is unwise to know that there is great temptation for inappropriate physical contact and yet to place oneself in a situation where resisting it will be tested.

---

37 Matthew 6:13

38 And if your right eye makes you stumble, tear it out, and throw it from you; for it is better for you that one of the parts of your body perish, than for your whole body to be thrown into hell. "And if your right hand makes you stumble, cut it off, and throw it from you; for it is better for you that one of the parts of your body perish, than for your whole body to go into hell. Matthew 5:29-30

It is very important that both the man and the woman involved in dating understand these dynamics. Ignorance by either is a recipe for trouble. Thus it is wise that Christians be careful of the impact that their dress, actions and demeanor may potentially have on the other person. Dating provides a dangerously ripe opportunity for laying strong and subtle temptation before another.

> *A young man asked his father if he could go to his girlfriend's home for the evening while her parents were out of town. When the father denied permission, the young man protested that the father did not trust him. To this the father replied, "I do not trust myself."*

His father understood the dynamics of two young people alone and unsupervised in a home. It is a potentially dangerous situation with which no one needs to be tempted.

Biblical Principles: Recognize your susceptibility to sin. Take the necessary steps to avoid falling into sin. Avoid and flee from temptation.

THOUGHT: How are you going to decide where to draw the line regarding physical contact during dating? Since physical contact leads only to a desire for more physical contact, then what level of physical contact is appropriate and pleasing to God? Since physical contact poses potential temptation, at what point will physical contact become a stumbling block causing the other person to sin? It would be very good to determine very conservative physical boundaries early in the relationship. No physical contact? Holding hands? Arm in arm? Casual kissing on the cheek?

Potential Dates = Potential Spouses

Many in the world would consider dating as a casual encounter to enjoy the other person's company. Others date to seek sexual encounters. For the Christian, dating should be purposeful and focused. Christian dating focuses only on determining whether or not an individual is a candidate for a lifetime marriage. If a person is ineligible for marriage due to spiritual, moral or any other lapse there is no reason to date them.

THOUGHT: If it becomes evident that the person you are dating is not "marriage" quality, what is the purpose in continuing dating? Dating that person should be discontinued immediately.

This is where the command not to be unequally yoked might relate to dating.[39] Marriage is binding, or "yoking," together by God. A yoke is the piece of wood or

---

39 1 Corinthians 6:14-18

metal that connects two oxen together so that they both pull the wagon or plow. If a small donkey is yoked together with a large oxen, they are unequally yoke and cannot pull together. If a Christian marries an unbeliever they are unequally bound or yoked together. The believer and unbeliever will have very different perspectives, worldviews, priorities and purposes in life. Since dating is a stepping stone leading to marriage, it is foolish to date someone whom you would not marry.

The most direct application of this Scripture is, of course, in regard to marrying unbelievers. Dating an unbeliever is a problem primarily because of where dating leads. If dating were only for friendship or for evangelistic purposes, then dating an unbeliever could be encouraged. However, this is not the case. Dating opens the door to emotional attachments, which often lead to marriage. Dating an unbeliever can (and often does) lead to marriage to an unbeliever. That is why it is widely held that believers should only date believers, although dating unbelievers is not explicitly prohibited in Scripture.

Christian in Name but Not in Nature

Being a believer, a Christian, a follower of Jesus, is more than making a verbal claim. Being a believer is living a life of faith in obedience to the Lord. The dating process should be used to evaluate carefully whether or not the profession of faith matches with the expected life of obedience. Many young men have professed faith in order to get his girl, only to fall aside shortly after the wedding.

Splinters in the Yoke

The principle of avoiding unequal yokes can be loosely applied in a greater scope. While the "great divide" of eligible marriage partners is having a common faith in Christ, there are many other aspects of individual lives that can constitute an unequal yoke.

Many problems in marriage may be avoided by ensuring that there are shared values and priorities in life. One does not have to look far in the Christian community to find a wide difference in priorities. For a successful marriage, both partners should be completely committed to the obedience of Christ in all areas of life. Marrying someone who seems weak or shallow in their relationship with Jesus may be marrying someone who does not know the Lord at all.

Additionally, a young lady should carefully evaluate the spiritual maturity of the man she is dating. Problems arise when a girl marries someone who is less spiritually mature than she is. The man is to be the spiritual leader in the family.[40] The difficulty of submitting to his leadership will be compounded if he is immature in the Lord. She also puts herself in a situation where she may feel

---

40   Ephesians 5:27

41

compelled to "lead" because she is more knowledgeable and mature. Additionally, the husband and father will be setting a spiritual tone in the family and an example for the children. Dating is the time to identify the spiritual maturity of the man and to make wise choices. After dating is over and the marriage has occurred options are few – mostly just "cope with it."

Like other aspects of dating, one's spiritual maturity can be portrayed to be something that it is not. Being Christians does not protect us from trying to make the best impression, showing our best side and being on our best behavior. Thus careful and prayerful discernment is needed to learn the spiritual condition of the other person.

Bright Red Flags

It is quite clear in Scripture that there are things of which God disapproves. Dating should be practiced in such a way to positively eliminate potential for their occurrence. On the short list would be things such as:

* Sexual intimacy outside of marriage.[41] Clear and conservative lines must be established and openly communicated regarding the extent of physical contact that will be acceptable in dating. An unwillingness to establish and abide by such lines is a clear indicator of the lack of respect for the other person and for God.

* Causing others to stumble.[42] Although a particular action may not be inherently sinful it may lead another to sin. The dress and action of women can easily provide a man with an open door for sinful thoughts.

- Disobedience to parents.[43] By the time dating age is reached an independent spirit has frequently also developed. To date a person contrary to the desires of one's parents is to disobey God. An individual willing to disobey God, and their parents, lacks humility. Their pride will make them a difficult person in marriage. Each person is expected to be in submission in marriage, the wife to the husband and the husband to the Lord. An unwillingness to be in submission to current authorities indicates a rebellious spirit is present. This will be a great source of problems in marriage. The issue is having a heart of submission. Even if parents are unreasonable, each child should desire and seek to submit to the fullest extent possible,[44] even though sometimes the child must reluctantly make independent decisions.

---

41 1 Thessalonians 4:3 for example.

42 Romans 14:13, 21; I Corinthians 8:9

43 Ephesians 6:1-3

44 1 Peter 2:18-3:8

Suggested Dating Guidelines

While it is not practical to give precise rules for all dating activities, there are some basic guidelines that may prove helpful in ensuring that your dating pleases God. Following these guidelines will so change the appearance of dating that some may say that it is not dating at all. These suggestions should provoke thought and consideration about the issues. As guidelines, they are open to individual adaptation. Additionally, each person should decide how to apply the principles behind the guidelines to specific situations.

The suggested guidelines are intended to help each person to think carefully in advance and to adopt some standards for dating that will be pleasing to God, before the moment of need arises. By deciding these things before you are date you will be able to make more objective, and probably better, decisions. Here are some suggested guidelines for dating:

Be Accountable. Parents should give permission for the date. They should approve time table, activity, destination, etc. In this way both people on the date are responsible to a third party regarding actions and punctuality. Thus, a young man becomes responsible to the girl's parents, not just to the girl. This provides a greater degree of motivation to do what is right.[45] While a 25 year old living on his own may be functionally "free" from his parents' direct supervision, it is still wise to be accountable to them.[46] Being accountable to another godly individual is another option. However, a word of caution. When choosing whom to be accountable to, young people may choose someone who will either be lenient or someone who only knows what they are told. This is not true accountability. The absence of accountability leaves the dating couple relying on their own strength to do what is right. This may result in sin that will leave guilt and sadness for a long time.

Accountability in dating can also be generally provided by dating in public settings and among people you know. "Crossing the line" almost always happens at times when the dating couple is isolated from people, especially from people who know them.

> THOUGHT: If it would be inappropriate to do what you are doing in a semi-private restaurant booth with people all around, then you probably should not be doing it.

---

45 The author requires that young men ask him for permission to take one of his daughters on a date. This relieves the girl of the pressure of having to say "no" when she does not want to go. Instead the father can say "no" for her. It also makes the young man very aware of his accountability to the father as well as the girl.

46 There may be a temptation to make yourself accountable to someone who only knows what you tell them. This type of accountability is really not accountability at all, but rather the appearance of accountability.

<u>Adopt a Potential Date Screening Criteria in Advance.</u> Everyone automatically does this to some extent. The suggestion here is that prior thought be given and specifics be identified in advance. Good decisions can be made more easily when a dating opportunity presents itself if criteria are determined in advance.

The purpose of dating is to screen candidates for marriage. Some people are not marriage candidates. Identify the minimum criteria of a mate. If a potential date does not meet the criteria, then don't date them. If you have not identified what you are looking for in a spouse, how will you know if the potential date possesses it or not?

To begin dating someone who you will not, or cannot marry is harmful to both parties since is creates emotional attachments and false expectations. If you don't apply objective criteria to potential dates, dating is haphazard and may lead to marrying someone you shouldn't. Even if the dating does not lead to marriage, the relationship will end in grief and pain. Without criteria one defaults to emotions or physical attraction as a basis for whom will be dated, neither of which are a good bases for such significant decisions.

> THOUGHT: Develop a checklist like the one below to evaluate potential dates before agreeing to go on a date. Ask an objective third party who possesses spiritual maturity to assist you in completing the checklist to reduce the tendency toward emotionally blinded responses.

Does the potential dating-marriage candidate possess the following qualities?

- Expresses a clear testimony of personal salvation.
- Has evidence of a Spiritual Life/Salvation (explain).
- Routinely reads/studies the Word of God? _____ hours/week
- Routinely spends time in prayer.   _____ hours/week
- Routinely attends church and enjoys it.   _____ hours/week
- Active in serving the Lord.   _____ hours/week
- Active in personal evangelism.
- Has a good understanding of basic spiritual truth.
- Demonstrates the fruit of the Spirit: love, joy, peace, patience, kindness, goodness, faithfulness, gentleness, self-control. (Gal 5:22-23)
- Obvious absence of the deeds of the flesh: immorality, impurity, sensuality, idolatry, involvement in spiritism, mysticism, sorcery, bitterness, conflict, jealousy, outbursts of anger, disputes, dissensions, divisions, envying, drunkenness, partying. (Gal. 5:19-21)
- Possesses a servant attitude.
- Demonstrates humility rather than pride.
- Admits to wrongs rather than excusing or hiding sin.
- Seeks forgiveness and reconciliation when aware of sin.

- Possesses a biblical view of marriage and divorce.

These are some sample questions that could be included. Identify criteria and include questions that are important to you. Obviously all of the questions cannot be answered with certainty when considering whether to date someone or not. However, negative answers to some of the questions should eliminate some people as potential candidates. A purposeful dating process will provide more accurate answers as time goes by and knowledge increases.

Implement a Dating Plan. A dating plan specifies how the purpose of dating - identifying a suitable spouse – will be accomplished. A dating plan is a guide that identifies priorities and goals in advance and how the goals will be accomplished. It is not necessarily a step by step dating procedure. Having a plan ensures that vitally important aspects are not omitted.

THOUGHT: A sample "DATING PLAN" may include:

A clearly articulated statement of your purpose in dating.
Clear criteria by which you will identify who you will date.
A statement of limits of physical contact (hold hands, arm in arm).
A statement of how to complete the screening process.
A statement of how you will get to know the other person's perspective on:
- finances,
- roles within marriage,
- political positions and view of government,
- views on children,
- spiritual commitment,
- views on divorce and remarriage,
- life goals and direction,
- baggage being carried (bad childhood or other relationships),
- views of work (workaholic or sloth), etc.
A statement of limits of places you will go and won't go.
Identifying people who will keep you accountable.

Developing and following a dating plan is really an exercise in self- discipline and forethought. It is the difference between living by faith based on the truth and living by emotions. By identifying and thinking about these things in advance one's dating experience will more likely be pleasant. Having a plan also will contribute significantly to finding a spouse who will be good and godly.

Treat the Other Person as You Would Treat Jesus. In dating, as in all other relationships between Christians, each person has a serious responsibility. The brother or sister in the Lord that we date is indwelt by the Spirit of God. How that person is treated is how the Lord is treated. Great care is needed to always do what is right and not sin against them.

Have a Pre-dating Deception Removal Discussion

> THOUGHT: Before agreeing to begin dating, clearly identify and discuss the purpose of dating with the person you are considering dating. Unless discussed it is unlikely that both will have the same assumptions about the purpose of dating. If the other person has a different purpose than you do in dating, then why date? How will you know their purpose unless you ask them and they tell you?

Very early in the relationship, clear the air about the intended goal and purpose of dating. Dating is a screening process for marriage. By having such a discussion up front, both parties will clearly understand the basis for their relationship.

If one party is not ready to marry, then what is the purpose of the date? If both parties are ready to marry and consider the other a potential candidate, then there is a basis for dating. This may seem unromantic. Yet the alternative is assumptions, misunderstandings, broken hearts and/or inappropriate behaviors.

A dating plan may include how to respond to someone who asks you out on a date. What will you say? How will you say it? When and how will you discuss the purpose of dating?

Typically people adopt a "wait and see" approach in dating rather than just putting the cards on the table. It is naturally awkward discussing such weighty and intimate issues. Imagine the exchange:

> Man: Would you like to go to dinner sometime?
> Woman: So, do you want to marry me or not?
> Man: uhhhhhh – like uhhhhh – how about a hamburger? Bye.
> Woman: Where did he go?

A more realistic approach when the prospect of a date arises and you are open to a dating relationship potentially leading to marriage might go something like this:

> "My perspective on dating is a bit different than many people. I have thought a lot about what would please God in dating. It seems to me that dating is a time to really get to know someone. I am not overly eager, but I think that dating is to see if there may be a potential for marriage in the future. What do you think about dating?"

Although it may be argued that it seems logical for a discussion about the purpose of dating occur only after there have been few dates, it usually does not get any easier. There are more problems with delaying the discussion than there are with the potential awkwardness of addressing it as a first priority. The problems include:

1. A pattern of dating becomes established before the discussion.
2. Budding emotional attachment increases the risks of the discussion.
3. Delaying the discussion sets up the other party to feel misled.
4. It is harder to backtrack than to not start down the path.
5. Care for the other person makes you not want to hurt them.

If you have adopted a clear purpose in dating, then you owe it to yourself, and to the other person, to be transparent about dating from the start.[47] Although it may be difficult, having the purpose discussion up front, will be best for everyone and honoring to God. How and when to have that discussion is something that can be included in a dating plan. As with many things in life, it is better to make clear your purpose in dating from the beginning rather than to try to fix a mess later because of different assumptions or purposes.

Obtain Permission and Talk to Others

When someone applies for a job they fill out applications and give references. When someone wants to rent an apartment they fill out applications and give references. Wise landlords and employers check references to validate their impression of the applicant.

> THOUGHT: Since marriage is a much greater commitment, with much more at stake than a job or house, wouldn't it be prudent to rely on someone more objective than your own impressions?

Dating often creates emotional attachments before getting to know the other person. Emotional attachments hinder seeing the person as they really are. Approaching dating in this way is counter-productive. A better approach is to get to know the person before building the emotional bonds.

To really get to know a person takes a long time and exposure to them in a variety of settings and circumstances. Dating usually happens in brief exposures, in limited circumstances, and over a relatively short time. So, to really get to know what a person is like, the help of other individuals will prove invaluable.

After agreeing that dating is a screening process for marriage, each person needs to learn everything they can about the other person. One way of effectively learning about the other person is to have open and frank discussion about them with other people who know them well.

Much can be learned about someone by talking to their parents, school teachers, siblings, pastors, employers and friends. These people usually have a good

---

47 If you don't have a clear purpose in dating, then you should identify one before dating.

understanding of the individual from different perspectives, in different settings and in different roles. They have had opportunities to see their strengths and weaknesses. By consulting with these types of people much more will be learned than might ever happen during typical "dating."

How to Learn About Your Date from Third Parties

1. Obtain and grant mutual permission to talk to third parties.
2. Prepare for the discussions by making a list of questions.
3. Explain to the third party the reason for your interest, the agreed purpose of dating and the permission you have obtained to have this discussion.
4. Ask them to be candid and given, the gravity of the situation. Candor and honesty does not need to exclude discretion.

Sample approach and questions:

As you may know, Jim and I are (considering) dating. Perhaps he has told you that he has given me his permission to ask you questions. We both agree that the purpose of dating is to find a life mate. Would you be willing to answer some questions for me about Jim? Please be completely honest. Jim and I plan to discuss the responses that you give. I will be talking to several people. Jim and I have agreed to keep the specific source of the information we receive confidential as best we can.

- *What is your opinion of Jim in general?*
- *What do you see as his strengths?*
- *What do you see as his weaknesses?*
- *What do you know of his family life?*
- *What do you think of his parents?*
- *What about Jim would make him a good husband? Father?*
- *What do you think Jim would struggle with as a husband? Father?*
- *What do you know of Jim's financial, work and time use habits?*
- *If you owned a business would you hire Jim for a responsible position? (Please explain)*
- *Would you want Jim to be your son-in-law? Why? Why not?*
- *What do you know of Jim's spiritual life? Saved, growing, serving?*
- *What kind of spiritual leadership would Jim provide in the family ?*
- *Is Jim willing to submit to authority?*
- *Has Jim ever been in trouble with school authorities or the law?*

- *What have been Jim's previous dating practices?*

These are sample questions. More or different questions can be asked. The goal is to learn as much about the other person as possible to determine who they are, what they are like and if you want to spend the rest of your life with them.

Being interviewed about a potential future spouse will likely be a new experience for most people. It may be an awkward experience for some people. This is a small price to be paid when the significance of marrying someone is considered.

Adopting any, or all of the suggestions offered will benefit you in dating. Even greater benefits will be realized in marriage. It is much better to get to say, "I am glad I never married him." than it is to say "I wished I had never married him." Dating is the gate that starts down the marriage road. Drawing upon all the resources available to start down the right road will make a great difference in your life.

Chapter 5
Choosing the Right Mate

<u>Resources for Assistance</u>

Choosing one's mate is for some a statement of their freedom from authority and independence from their parents. The price for making such a statement may be much greater than any benefit gained. To make such a significant lifetime decision, without the input of others, may have detrimental impact on the rest of your life.

As with other areas of life, God has put people in our lives to help us make good decisions including identification of a suitable mate. It is unwise to reject God's provision for help, simply because we are a "big boy and can do it ourselves!"

Parents are God's first source for assistance available when choosing a spouse. The more godly the parents, the greater the benefit their counsel and advice will be. Regardless of their spiritual state though, parents frequently offer a perspective of experience and insight that is very valuable. Even though someone's parents may have made a mess of their own lives, they have learned lessons that can help their children avoid falling into the same pit. God's command to "honor your father and mother" is independent of their honorableness and is not age related. Children honor their parents by seeking their counsel regarding dating and marriage.[48]

Since your potential marriage partner is of the opposite sex there are some natural barriers to understanding them. This is true in life, in dating and in marriage. To some extent, men understand men and women understand women because their thinking, emotions and methodologies are similar. Much insight into the character of a potential spouse can be gained by conversing with those who see them from within their same gender pool.

This is not what is normally done. The natural tendency is for girls to talk about boys they are interested in with their mother, sisters or other girls. Boys normally . . . well they naturally don't talk much about girls at all – at least not appropriately.

---

48   It is important that parents be consulted in the very early stages of the dating process. Sometimes parents are not consulted until after emotional bonds have occurred and decisions have been made. By this time children are often simply asking for acceptance of their decisions not counsel or advice. When the child has already made the decision and the parent offers counsel that is contrary to the decision, the counsel is often unwisely rejected and resented.

However, when fathers spend time in serious conversation with any potential son-in-law, they can provide daughters with much insight into their character. Similarly, mothers who spend time with a potential daughter-in-law will be able to offer her son insight that neither the father nor son may be able to see on their own. Men are better able to "see through" men and women are better able to "see through" women. Parental input should be a significant factor in assessing a potential spouse.

Pastors and church leaders offer another source of effective input into decision making regarding marriage partners. Godly leaders can help a young person to consider what the Bible says about dating and marriage well in advance of being ready to date. Adopting a biblical perspective can be established before emotions cloud judgment and hinders understanding.

A good rapport with a pastor enables the young person to bring questions to him throughout the dating process. After two people have decided to marry, the pastor can also provide counsel and guidance. This guidance can come in the way of practical exercises to work out some of the overlooked details of marriage.

Factors to Criteria

Biblically there is one, and only one, criteria for who the Christian can and cannot marry. The Christian is to marry another Christian – they are not to be "unequally yoked." However, there are other factors that will impact the nature of the marriage relationship. These factors need to be given some thought and consideration before and throughout the dating process.

Compatibility

Sometimes it is asserted that the purpose of dating is to "find out if two people are compatible."[49] In some ways, compatibility is a myth. No two people are compatible. By nature, each person is self-centered, selfish, self-willed and inclined to seek their own needs while disregarding the needs of others. To think that two such people placed under the same roof, sharing one bathroom and one bank account would be compatible is laughable. Instead, it is a formula for disaster.

On the other hand, there is a sense in which no two Christians are incompatible. If both are saved, if both have the mind of Christ, if both are willing to submit to God, if both love others as Christ loved them and gave Himself for them, then they will have no problems. Compatibility in a genuine "Christian" marriage is not an issue. If both people are saved and if they are committed to God they are compatible. (Note the number of "ifs" in this paragraph.)

---

49   Some even take this to the extreme of experimenting with whether they are sexually compatible. This is a blatantly sinful practice.

Although universal Christian compatibility may sound like "pie in the sky" theology, it is a very practical truth. Two people unified in Christ, grow closer together as each one grows closer to Christ. So, in this sense, one can say that being a committed believer is the only compatibility requirement. Of course, "committed" should be an unnecessary word when placed alongside the word "Christian." But in Christendom there are many so-called "Christians" who are not committed. Indeed, there are many who would attach the name "Christian" to themselves when they are not followers of Jesus in any way at all. Those who are true disciples of Jesus, though, usually live and breathe somewhere between the two ends of the spectrum. Commitment fluctuates depending on one's daily relationship with the Lord. This makes the discussion of compatibility more pertinent. There are lots of differences and factors to be considered regarding potential spouses.

<u>Preferences and Barriers</u>

Many of the "compatibility" considerations fall more into the categories of personal preferences and practicality rather than being right or wrong. There are numerous barriers in the world that cause interpersonal relationships to be especially difficult. If brought into marriage, these barriers will create additional challenges that would not exist in their absence. The greater the number or intensity of these barriers, the greater potential for misunderstanding and difficulty in the marriage. Thus, it is prudent to be aware of existing and potential barriers prior to entering into marriage.

<u>Social-Economic Barriers.</u> Each person is accustomed to some standard of living. When people marry, they will bring expectations regarding income, lifestyle, availability of funds, etc., into the relationship. The greater the difference in background and perspective in these areas, the more divergent the expectations will be and the greater the potential for problems. The greater the difference in social-economic status and lifestyle, the greater the potential for misunderstanding and strain on the relationship.

<u>Cultural Barriers.</u> Cross cultural[50] marriages require greater effort than marriages within the same culture. "Cross cultural" includes more subtle differences than language, dress and traditions arising from different nationalities. Cross cultural differences arise from sub-cultures of many kinds such as the city folk and the country bumpkin.

Indeed, each family has a culture of its own. Each marriage partner brings elements of their upbringing and family background into marriage, and there will be bumps in the marriage because of it. However, the greater the cultural differences, the more potential for bumps, misunderstanding and problems. Thus,

---

50 The Bible contains no prohibitions against inter-racial marriages, although some would wrongly claim that it does.

more effort will be required within the marriage when more, and greater cultural differences exist between marriage partners.

Religious Barriers. Just because two people are Christians does not mean that they do not have religious differences. Denominational (or non-denominational) variations, distinctions and practices offer potential for problems. Religious customs, practices and traditions vary from church to church and from pastor to pastor. Each believer has a set of expectations regarding church buildings, church programs, sermon styles, music styles, church leadership, pastoral visitation, service involvement, etc. The greater the differences in Christian background, the greater the potential for dissatisfaction, disagreement and conflict.

Family Role Barriers. The expectation brought into a marriage by each partner is usually that their spouse will fulfill duties and responsibilities as their own mother and father did. Since there are many duties that either father or mother may assume, there is frequently a wide variation between families. This is not a matter of biblically defined roles but one of practical family life. Variations include who takes out trash, who mows grass, who pays bills, etc. Family roles also include employment status and activity status of the parents. Do both parents work? Or only one? Which one? What does the other parent do? Some of these roles and functions are cultural and can be a source of tension. Some roles and functions are based on biblical principles, but many others are not.

Family History Barriers. Some people have had good role models in their life and others have not. A person raised in a single parent home will have a vastly different view of life and marriage than one raised with two parents. A family where both parents are Christians will have different dynamics than one in which only one parent is a Christian. The interaction between marriage partners is also significantly different when only one of the parents is a committed Christian. If a prospective spouse experienced a different type of family, there will be the related differences that have broad implications. For example, a boy raised by his mother may have lacked the male role model in his life. Associated with that lack, his understanding of how to treat a wife, and how to be a father, may be limited or lacking. Differences in family history need to be identified and addressed.

Personal Barriers. By the time marriage occurs, many people have already lived nearly one-third of their lives. They bring with them a history, some of which is easily exchanged or discarded and others that linger indefinitely. These may include, but are not limited to, alcohol or drug abuse, sexual promiscuity, gambling, pornography, lack of self-control in various areas, eating disorders, excesses of various kinds, debt, sloth, laziness, and on and on. These matters can be considered as personal cultural barriers. When people come into marriage with history, and everyone does, the baggage has to be carried by both people in the relationship. The key to overcoming the barriers depends largely in identifying them. Once identified, barriers can be resolved, or at least dealt with appropriately and biblically as they arise.

Although none of these compatibility issues are necessarily prohibitive, they all merit conscious consideration. The best time to consider them is before dating begins. Aware that greater differences between people creates greater potential for conflict and struggle, a dating plan can include ways to identify these types of differences. The plan should include how to determine which barriers are prohibitive and how to resolve those that can be accepted and tolerated.

In spite of all the "differences" that may exist, the key to compatibility is a selfless devotion to Jesus Christ by both marriage partners. When each partner is unreservedly committed to serving God then all the other barriers can be overcome. Being a Christian does not eliminate the differences, but it does provide the tools to work through them. Some differences are easily resolved and others require greater effort.

<u>Is Dating Excluded?</u>

Although dating poses many potential problems and pitfalls, they can be avoided. Dating should be carefully and prayerfully crafted to please God and protect yourself and others from sin. The dating of the world is not pleasing to God for numerous reasons. The person serious about pleasing the Lord and doing what is right will understand the purpose and practice of dating very differently than the unbeliever. Dating should not be something that "just happens." God cares about who and how you date.

Those who advocate courting as biblical and condemn dating as un-biblical do so based on cultural grounds than on biblical grounds. Whether one "courts" or "dates" is of little significance, if a person follows the principles in the Bible. Indeed, the principles and guidelines laid out above probably are closer to what would be considered "courting" than "dating" but this is just preference in words.

This book is not intended to be a complete guide to dating. Rather it should serve as a brain tickler, a guiding light, and perhaps a stimulation to think carefully. Hopefully you have found some food for thought as you have considered dating and how it pertains to you. Take time and prayerfully consider if, when, and how you will date so that God is glorified in all areas of your life.

Chapter 6

Modesty, Flirting and Attraction

Defining Modesty

Perhaps surprisingly, there is only one place in the Bible where a form of the word modest occurs.

> Likewise, I want women to adorn themselves with proper clothing, modestly and discreetly, not with braided hair and gold or pearls or costly garments, but rather by means of good works, as is proper for women making a claim to godliness. (1 Timothy 2:9-10)[51]

The use of the word "modestly" is parallel to the word "discreetly" and both terms are describing "proper clothing." The emphasis in this text, as in others,[52] is on the inner quality of the heart. However, the issue of appearance is addressed because so much emphasis is often placed upon outward beauty.

A broader look at his text reveals that the instructions given to women falls in the larger context of all Christians having a proper attitude of submission to authority:

- 1 Timothy 2:1-7 - pray for leaders.
- 1 Timothy 2:8 - Men pray with holiness, in submission, instead of having wrath and dissension.
- 1 Timothy 3:1ff – qualifications for church leaders.

Modesty then, and specifically modest dressing, is somehow related to the right attitude of submission to authority. Another passage that focuses on what women wear also occurs in the context of a serious discussion about submission. Peter, speaking about doing what is right and suffering for it while submitting to authority, addresses women's apparel.

> Your adornment must not be merely external -- braiding the hair, and wearing gold jewelry, or putting on dresses; but let it be the hidden person of the heart, with the imperishable quality of a gentle and quiet spirit, which is precious in the sight of God. For in this way in former times the holy women also, who hoped in God, used to adorn themselves, being submissive to their own husbands; (1 Peter 3:3-5)

---

51   The NIV and NKJ versions also use the word in 1 Corinthians 12:23

52   For example see 1 Peter 3:3-5 and Proverbs 31:30, Charm is deceitful and beauty is vain but a woman who fears the LORD, she shall be praised.

At the heart of modesty is a humble and submissive attitude. Immodesty then arises out of a proud and rebellious attitude. Not surprisingly, Proverbs describes the character of the seductive and adulterous woman as "boisterous and rebellious."[53]

Modesty is an attitude of submission that expresses itself in many ways including one's speech, behavior, apparel and appearance. Modesty is related to flirting. In many instances, physical or verbal immodesty is a type of flirting that is sexually provocative.

Even dictionary definitions of modesty includes underlying attitudes of humility and submission expressed in certain behaviors. The definition of "modest" includes:

- placing a moderate estimate on one's abilities or worth
- neither bold nor self-assertive
- observing the proprieties of dress and behavior

Assessment of Modesty

The submission and humility in modesty is first and foremost in one's relationship with God. God is the one who defines what is right and appropriate. The modest person humbly accepts what God says and willingly submits to God.

Modesty includes one's dress, yet the heart of the issue goes much deeper than one's physical appearance. This attitude of the heart expresses itself outward behavior and appearance. Modesty is, at its core, submission to God. It is also submission to those whom He delegates His authority.

> Ester put on two layers of clothes as she prepared to go to school. The outer layer would certainly meet her parents' approval. Upon arriving at school, however, the layer she never would be let out of the house with was revealed, a spaghetti strap tank top. The sweatshirt was tossed into her locker. By changing clothes at school to the outfit she knew her father would disapprove of, she was rebellious, and therefore, she was immodest.

So what is modest apparel and what is immodest? Drawing thin dark lines to mark the boundaries between modesty and immodesty is difficult. Yet the person who seeks to please God will not try to define lines and then to push the boundaries. However, here are some guidelines that may help evaluate dress, speech and behaviors regarding modesty:

---

53 Proverbs 7:11

- Modesty covers the body.
  - The definition of "sufficient covering" is determined by those who are seeing the clothes, not by those who are wearing them.
  - Exposing any portion of breasts, genitals, or excessive skin is immodest.
  - Clothing may be immodest because it is too tight or too loose or suggestive.
  - If clothing is revealing such that it may provoke lustful thoughts by a member of the opposite sex, then it is not sufficient.
  - Different bodies are different. What is modest on one person may be immodest on another.
- If clothing is sexy, it is immodest.
  - "Sexy" means that it provokes thoughts of sexual activity.
  - Clothing, or accessories, that draw sexually related attention to the body are sexy, and therefore inappropriate. This would include low cut tops, low cut jeans, slits in skirts or dresses, tight fitting apparel, strategically placed necklaces or broaches, etc.
  - Logos, words, pictures, patches or patterns on clothing may be immodest because they attract inappropriate attention to parts of the body.
  - Of course, being sexy within the marriage relationship is appropriate in private.
- Modesty recognizes that your body belongs first to God and then to your spouse (if you have one).
  - Putting your body on display is not an individual right.
  - Provocative dress is sinful flirting, exposing and offering views of your body that are reserved for your spouse.

The word that is translated "discreetly" or "propriety" in 1 Timothy 2:9 means to have sound judgment and to behave with a thoughtful awareness of what is best. Modesty is recognizing the implications for behavior and dress as they relate to submission to God and doing what is best for those around you.

Modesty and being attractive are related. Scripture acknowledges that the world's attractiveness is outward but that true beauty arises from the character of the heart. Immodesty is a heart issue that is revealed and associated with flirting.

Flirting

The secretary opened the door for the job applicant, rolled her eyes, and returned to her desk. She was appalled. The applicant, "dressed to kill" in a short, tight fitting, low-cut dress, had giggled, fluttered her eyes, and took the few short steps to her seat with exaggerated sways of her hips. It was obvious that the woman was hoping that her flirtations would increase her chances of landing the job. The secretary sighed out loud, "Good thing a man is interviewing her instead of me." The other applicants in the waiting room could not conceal their snickers.

Not all flirting is so blatant nor intentional.

Renee was as embarrassed as she was confused as she returned to join her group of friends. Her father had called her away abruptly, reprimanded her harshly for flirting and sent her on her way. Under her breath she mumbled, shaking her head slowly from side to side, "Flirting? I was not flirting. What did I do that he thought was flirting?"

Renee's father had a different perspective, of course. What he had observed startled and surprised him. His response was more instinctive than thought out. Her father's account would be more like this:

"Renee!" The frustration and impatience was obvious in her father's voice. "Come here!" Reluctantly, with a sigh, grimace, toss of the hair and eyes rolling far back into her head, Renee left her mixed group of friends and approached her dad.

Renee's father carefully faced away from the group. He motioned for her to come around and face him. Careful to not allow her peers to overhear, Renee's father revealed the nature of his summons. "Renee, you are blatantly flirting. This is unacceptable behavior!" Twelve year old Renee, looked up at her father with wrinkled nose and head cocked to one side confused, flabbergasted and a bit embarrassed. The measured words slowly slipped from her mouth in a barely audible tone that evidenced she believed them with all her heart even though she was not exactly sure what flirting was, "I . . . am . . . not . . . flirting." Her father, jutting his head toward her while raising his shoulders nearly to his ears, obviously disagreed, "Go on. We will talk later. But, pleeeeeeease . . . think about what you are doing."

Some common behaviors in life are frequently assumed to be acceptable simply because they are prevalent and pervasive. In relationships with the opposite sex, immodesty, striving to be attractive and flirting are expressed in all cultures to some degree because they are part of human nature. But even though attractiveness, immodesty and flirting are prevalent in the world, they have moral implications. Each of these need to be given some thoughtful consideration as they relate to dating and marriage.

Renee's father thought she was flirting. Renee disagreed. The same story could focus on modesty, instead of flirting, with the same result. The father may think Renee was being immodest. Renee may disagree. A common complaint goes something like this, "My father wants me to be homely and ugly. I just want to be attractive. I just want to fit in. If he had his way I would have to wear a burka."

Why the great difference in perspectives? Is it a father-daughter difference? Is it a male-female difference? Is it a teen-adult issue? Who, is right? Are both right in some ways? Are these issues just unimportant matters of preference? Do the differences matter?

These questions, and similar ones, can be answered by first defining the issues and then consulting the Bible to gain God's perspective.

<u>Defining Flirting</u>

What does it mean to flirt? Dictionary definitions include:
- To make playfully romantic or sexual overtures.
- To deal playfully, trifling, or superficially with another

The basic idea of flirting is:
- to toy with something,
- to offer the hope of something without actually offering,
- to suggest something without fully expressing it,
- to make an approach toward something without intending necessarily to follow through.

Although the meaning of the word flirt can apply broadly to many different areas of life, its most prevalent uses relate to the interaction between two people of the opposite sex. As such, flirting is an expression of a playful and teasing interest in another person. Flirting tells the other person that a door is open, at least a little bit, with an implied invitation for them to peek through and to pursue more interaction of some kind. Flirting may solicit increased interaction ranging from a willingness to have additional casual conversation or it may be opening the door to a sexual encounter or anything in between. Flirting may also just be suggestive in order to tease without any thought of anything more than the tease itself.

Some people think it is fun to flirt, kind of a game to be played. One website listing 101 ways to flirt says, "If you want to attract attention from the opposite sex or just have some fun, this list of 101 ways to flirt will give you plenty of ideas to get started."[54]

---

54   http://dating.lovetoknow.com/List_of_101_Ways_to_Flirt

Some would suggest that flirting is an innocent common practice that is neither inappropriate nor wrong. But those who want to please God should consider the matter carefully and thoughtfully.

Flirting, by nature, is indistinct, vague and open to a wide range of interpretations. The message communicated in flirting depends on the people involved, the setting, their backgrounds and their character. To a 12 year old girl, flirting may simply be viewed as having fun with a group of friends laughing and giggling and smiling and joking. But to the 18 year old "worldly wise" boy in the group, that "innocent" flirting may be perceived as a willingness and an invitation to "go all the way." In the extreme, a boy may hear a girl say the words "no" and "stop," but because of previous teasing and flirting, he may wrongly assume that the girl is still teasing and ignore her objections to his advances. This is **not** to suggest in any way that such a boy's behavior is excusable. But sometimes communication is complicated. Flirting, by nature is non-definitive and is open to a wide range of interpretations. What is intended by the one doing the flirting can easily be misunderstood by the one interpreting what the flirting means.

A website giving advice about how to flirt says, *"Don't take it too seriously. Keep in mind that flirting is supposed to be fun, and try not to be crushed if your efforts aren't successful — not every interaction will be a perfect 10. Stay positive, and try again with someone else. As with anything else, flirting improves with practice."*

According to this site "successful flirting" scores a date, or scores an intimate encounter.[55] Many websites affirm that flirting is related to initiating some level of relationship with the opposite sex, particularly soliciting a date or anything included in the world's perspective on dating.

Flirting can be expressed in many different ways - asking a question, initiating conversation, paying a compliment, making eye contact, glancing, staring, smiling, joking, giving a look, teasing, playing coy or pretending to be uninterested, etc. Almost anything can be flirting. Almost anything can be perceived as flirting whether it was intended to be or not. Flirting can be expressed in words, gestures, facial expression, clothing, other body language, etc. In the case of Renee, her father and perhaps others saw her flirting when apparently she had no conscious intent to flirt. So what makes and action flirting?

<u>Pondering and Clarifying Flirting</u>

The word flirt is a verb, referring to the act of flirting but it also can be used as a noun. A person who frequently, habitually, or indiscriminately flirts is sometimes labeled "a flirt." To be a flirt is usually looked down upon, even in today's promiscuous culture. A "flirt" is one who flirts without discretion, teasing and

---

55   http://www.wikihow.com/Flirt

playfully interacting with any and every person of the opposite sex who crosses their path. The disdain for a flirt probably arises in part from the fact that many of those being teased are unavailable. Most people consider it inappropriate to have someone make a play for an unavailable person, even casually. The flirt is usually more interested in teasing and taunting than actually following through on their implied suggestions or promises. Flirting arouses an interest and a desire in the other person that gives the flirt a sense of self satisfaction that they are either in control, attractive or desirable to the other person.

To better understand flirting, it may be helpful to ask, "What is the opposite of flirting?" It seems to be a simple question: yet, the answer does not come easily. Perhaps it would be easier to ask, "What is the opposite of being flirtatious?" This too seems difficult to define. Some words, and behaviors, do not have opposites. However, what can be expressed is the <u>absence</u> of being flirtatious.

A non-flirtatious person is one who respectfully interacts with the opposite sex without suggesting or inviting inappropriate interest (romantic, sexual, or otherwise) in them in any way.

This definition has several components that define the non-flirtatious person and can be helpful in understanding flirting.
- They do interact with members of the opposite sex.
  - A person does not need to be cold, aloof, shunning or shy in order to avoid flirting.
- They are respectful of the other person.
  - They are concerned about the other person more than themselves, their own ego or their own self-gratification.
- Their interaction is not romantically or sexually motivated.
- Their interaction does not invite romantic or sexual interest.

A person can be kind, reasonably attentive and conversant with a person of the opposite sex without flirting. Avoiding flirtation does not mean a person has to be cold, aloof, rude, shy or disengaged. The non-flirtatious person simply controls their words and actions so that they do not suggest or invite romantic or sexual interest. They are modest and appropriate in every way and therefore not sexually "provocative." They avoid provoking inappropriate interest in themselves.

Assessment of Flirting

So is flirting right or wrong? Does flirting have moral significance? Is it wrong to flirt at times and perhaps acceptable at other times? Some of these questions can be answered clearly and other are more difficult.

It should not have to be argued that if someone is married, it is wrong for them to engage in flirting with anyone other than their spouse. Marriage is a mutually exclusive relationship. Marriage excludes inviting another person to enter into a romantic, intimate or sexual relationship. Within the marriage relationship, flirting may be more accurately called sexual foreplay. It is still flirting, but the promise extended in the suggestions and teasing can be legitimately and appropriately fulfilled within marriage.

Flirting is also wrong when it causes another person to sin. If flirting provokes impure thoughts in another person, both people have sinned.[56] The person with the impure thoughts has sinned,and the person who created the situation that gave rise to impure thoughts, share in the guilt. The Bible uses the picture of a stumbling block. One person places the block and the other person falls over it. Becoming a stumbling block for another person is a serious sin repeatedly warned against in Scripture. For example:

> Therefore let us not judge one another anymore, but rather determine this - not to put an obstacle or a stumbling block in a brother's way.
> (Romans 14:13)

> but whoever causes one of these little ones who believe in Me to stumble, it would be better for him to have a heavy millstone hung around his neck, and to be drowned in the depth of the sea. Woe to the world because of its stumbling blocks! For it is inevitable that stumbling blocks come; but woe to that man through whom the stumbling block comes!
> (Matthew 18:6-7)

Flirting is also wrong whenever it extends or implies a promise that cannot be kept, or when there is no intention to keep it. The majority of flirting would fall in this category. Most flirting is making suggestions without any intent to follow through. This is part of the reason for the disdain that is directed toward one who is a "flirt." The flirt is flaunting themselves, teasing and taunting but has no intent for the relationship to go anywhere. They are just "having fun" at the expense of the other person. Additionally, when those who are not open for dating or marriage flirt, they are extending offers that they do not intend to follow through on. Flirting in this case is a deception based on a lie. Lying and deceiving are sins which are clearly condemned by God.

Although the term flirting is absent[57] from most translations of the Bible, the concept is quite prevalent in the book of Proverbs in discussions about the "strange woman" who is a prostitute. The flattering words, suggestive looks and immodest apparel of the strange woman all are means of flirting that young men are warned to avoid.

---

56 Matthew 5:28 but I say to you that everyone who looks at a woman with lust for her has already committed adultery with her in his heart.

57 The NIV translation of Isaiah 3:16 includes the word "flirting:" "The LORD says, "The women of Zion are haughty, walking along with outstretched necks, flirting with their eyes, tripping along with mincing steps, with ornaments jingling on their ankles." Other translations use the word seductive or wanton.

Can Flirting Ever Be Acceptable?

It has already been acknowledged that flirting within marriage is acceptable because of the relationship that exists and the dynamics of that relationship. A husband or wife can suggest romance and intimacy directed toward one another because their relationship is acceptable to God, and they can legitimately follow through on their promises.

Additionally, there may be other instances in which flirting may be acceptable, providing it does not include anything that is inappropriate and displeasing to God in intent and extent. Fundamentally, flirting is a means of communicating an openness to a closer relationship with another person of the opposite sex. If the potential relationship is acceptable, and the means of communication are acceptable, then the flirting is acceptable. For example, instances of flirting may occur in interaction between two Christian young people as a means of communicating a willingness to possibly date the other person. For the flirting to be acceptable, the extent of the intended relationship would have to be pleasing to God and the means of communicating would have to be pleasing to God. In this way, it is possible that these two young people could joke, tease and laugh together – technically flirting – without being inappropriate. Flirting would be a means of communicating a willingness to transition from a casual friendship or acquaintance into a dating relationship with an assessment for future marriage as the goal.

This same type of interaction would not be appropriate if either of the two people involved are not "eligible" because one is married, or because they have no interest in being married or are too young to marry.

The book Song of Solomon describes a relationship between a man and woman that includes flirting of all sorts within the bounds of an engagement leading to an eventual marriage. Flirting in this case is in anticipation of the marriage, maybe the equivalent of being engaged to be married. Three times in this book there is the admonition, "That you do not arouse or awaken *my* love until she pleases." Caution and care is needed to ensure that flirting does not result in compromising behavior outside of the marriage relationship.

In the case of Renee, it is safe to assume that since she is not ready to marry at 12 years old, then there is no need for a dating relationship. Thus, if she did flirt, it would be suggesting a relationship that would not be possible at this time and it would be inappropriate for such a relationship to occur. It is quite possible that Renee was unwittingly flirting and her father would recognize it because of life experience that Renee lacked.

Because flirting is so prevalent in immoral societies and frequently portrayed as normal and acceptable, it is easy to fail to see it for what it is. Christians need to think carefully about flirting to ensure that they don't send the wrong message and, more importantly, that they are pleasing to God.

Christians can strive to not flirt with others, but it is not as easy to avoid having someone flirt with you. When someone flirts with you it is naturally flattering. The person has interest in you, perhaps considers you attractive or has a desire to be with you. An appropriate biblical response to inappropriate flirting includes:

- Avoid flirting in return which encourages more flirting.
- Keep your interactions brief, focused, and appropriate.
- Put distance between yourself and the person flirting.

Inappropriate flirting frequently occurs through immodesty in dress, communication or behavior. Society places emphasis and value upon being attractive. Unwittingly, many Christians adopt the world's view of being attractive rather than God's view. The world's view of attractiveness often includes immodest and sinful flirtation.

Defining Attractive

> *"Dad, may I wear makeup?" asks 13 year old Bradie. Dad replies, "Bradie, you are my beautiful darling. Why do you want to wear make up?" "Mom wears make up. A lot of my friends wear makeup." she offers. "Sure they do. But I am asking why you want to wear makeup." Dad presses the issue. Frustrated, Bradie pleads, "Dad! I want to be attractive. Make up makes girls attractive. That is why I want to wear it! May I wear makeup, or do you want me to be ugly?"*

The word "attractive" is so common in the world that few people actually pause to think about what the word means. It is not a complicated word, and the meaning of the word is apparent. To be attractive means to attract something. To do something with the intent to become more attractive means to increase the likelihood that you will be noticed.

Dictionaries define attractive as:

- Having the power to attract.
- Pleasing to the eye or mind; charming.
- Appealing to senses or mind through beauty, form, character, etc.
- Arousing interest.
- Possessing the ability to draw or pull.

No father desires that his daughter be ugly, to be sure. But what father thinks it a good idea for his little girl to have the power to attract, to be pleasing to the eye and appealing to the senses through form or beauty? Certainly a time will come when being attractive will play a part in the girl's life, but that time should not be when she is years away from being ready to marry.

Being attractive has an inherently sexual aspect. To a large extent, the terms "attractive" and "sexy" are used interchangeably. "Attractive" is a sanitized synonym for the word "sexy." To be sexy means to be attractive and desirable for the purpose of sex. The dictionary defines, and it is generally understood that, being sexy is "exciting, or intending to excite, sexual desires; erotic." Some may assert that being attractive is not the same as being sexy. If so, then what are they trying to attract? Is it that being attractive is slightly "sexy," and being sexy is being really "SEXY!?" If the distinction between being attractive and being sexy is a matter of degrees, then where is the line?

These questions are being posed to help the reader think about underlying issues of the heart. It is so easy to simply adopt the way of the world and go with the flow; and yet, it is so important to think about what is being done and why it is being done if the goal is to be pleasing to God.

How does being "attractive" relate to biblically appropriate modesty? How does being attractive relate to flirting? When a girl or woman arranges her hair, puts on make-up, chooses her clothing intentionally to appear attractive, what are the implications? Who is she trying to attract and why?

In the Bible the emphasis is fostering in inner person beauty and attractiveness.

> Likewise, I want women to adorn themselves with proper clothing, modestly and discreetly, not with braided hair and gold or pearls or costly garments, but rather <u>by means of good works, as is proper for women making a claim to godliness</u>. (1 Timothy 2:9-10 emphasis added)

> Your adornment must not be *merely* external - braiding the hair, and wearing gold jewelry, or putting on dresses; <u>but let it be the hidden person of the heart, with the imperishable quality of a gentle and quiet spirit, which is precious in the sight of God</u>. (1 Peter 3:3-4 emphasis added)

Christians also need to guard their hearts and deal appropriately when they feel attracted to someone or are sexually excited by someone. God gives specific instructions regarding these things.

> Now flee from youthful lusts and pursue righteousness, faith, love and peace, with those who call on the Lord from a pure heart. (2 Timothy 2:22)

Similarly, 1 Corinthians 6:18 says to flee immorality. The Christian is to avoid temptation and flee from it when it occurs.

65

Stages of Life Do Matter

Robin (12) and Rex (13) had grown up together. They were friends at church, and they attended the same classes at Sunday School and VBS. Their families had outings together and spent time together. Robin and Rex played together. One day, out of the blue, Robin's parents sat her down and began to give her a lecture about flirting. Specifically, she was instructed about not flirting with Rex. Robin was confused. She and Rex were forever friends. They were just doing what they had been doing for the last ten years – playing, laughing, joking, roughhousing, teasing and sometimes quarreling. Why was it now a problem when it was never a problem before? What had changed?

What had changed was Robin and Rex. Time had passed, puberty had come, and the two childhood friends now were adolescents. The same behaviors that had previously been innocent childish play were now potentially sexually arousing interactions between the two young people.

Often parents are as surprised by this transition as are their children. One day it happens. A parent observes their child and thinks, "he/she is flirting!" A few months earlier the same behavior would have been observed, taken in stride and no thought given to the interaction. But as the child matures toward adulthood the normal transition changes the way behaviors are viewed, usually first by the parent, and eventually by the child. These changes often become a source of tension between parent and child because, although both see things differently than before, they do not necessarily agree on what is the appropriate response to the changes. Anticipating and discussing the changes in advance will help. Patience and humility will also promote peace and harmony.

Careful consideration needs to be given to the issues of modesty, flirting and attractiveness. God cares about each of these things and the person desiring to please God will adopt God's perspective rather than the world's viewpoint on these issues. People often want to draw lines, make rules regarding these matters, and focus on the exterior. But, God is more concerned about the heart. Instead of trying to get as close as possible to some artificially created line, the heart that seeks God will avoid any appearance of approaching the lines.

Chapter 7
Singleness: Unhindered Service

Being single is a tremendous blessing for some. For others, it is a constant nagging struggle. There are numerous reasons why people do not marry. Some reasons are good. Others are, perhaps, not so good.

> *The bride tottered down the aisle, her thin gray hair neatly combed and her sunken, withered cheeks cracked in smiles. She approached her bald toothless groom who awaited resting on two stout crutches, steadied by the best man. "Why did such old people ever fall for each other?" whispered a spectator. "Oh, they have been engaged since they were nineteen," replied another, "but they just waited until they could afford to be married."*

Then...

> *The old bachelor was smitten with Jane Smith who had also never married. Being unable to muster the courage to pop the question in person, he decided to do it by telephone. "Miss Smith?" he inquired. "Speaking." was the reply. He still struggled to get the words to come, "Will, uh, er, you, ah, marry me?" "Why, of course," replied Jane instantly. "Who is this please?"*

Then...

> *All of the girl's friends had married and they were chiding her about her single state. "Oh, lay off!" she snapped at last. "I'll have you know that I can marry any man I please." "Oh, yeah?" retorted one of the others. "Why don't you then?" "Because," she whispered, "I don't seem to please anyone."*

While there are many humorous stories associated with being "old maids" and "confirmed bachelors," being single is indeed a very personal and a very important matter. The Bible addresses singleness and provides understanding of God's perspective. Marriage is the prevalent human experience in life and in the Scriptures. Singleness is the exception. Even though singleness is the exception, it is not an inferior state. According to the Bible, being single provides some significant advantages over being married.

Singleness is Not For All

As recorded in Matthew's gospel account, Jesus made some very strong statements about God's perspective on marriage, adultery and divorce. In response to Jesus' teachings, the disciples suggested that singleness would be preferable.

"If the relationship of the man with his wife is like this, it is better not to marry." Matthew 19:10[58]

In response to their suggestion, Jesus asserted:

. . . "Not all men {can} accept this statement, but {only} those to whom it has been given. For there are eunuchs who were born that way from their mother's womb; and there are eunuchs who were made eunuchs by men; and there are {also} eunuchs who made themselves eunuchs for the sake of the kingdom of heaven. He who is able to accept {this,} let him accept {it."} Matthew 19:10-12[59]

This dialogue between the disciples and Jesus came in the course of a discussion about divorce initiated when some Pharisees asked, "Is it lawful {for a man} to divorce his wife for any cause at all? Jesus' response provoked another question from the Pharisees regarding why Moses had commanded the issuing of divorce certificates. Jesus answered this question by saying in part, that whoever divorces his wife, except for immorality, and marries another woman commits adultery.[60]

The disciples concluded that if the only options are to stay married or become guilty of adultery, then it would be better not to marry at all.

Jesus countered that "not to marry" is an option for some but not for everyone. He said that it is for {only} those to whom it has been given. He said that singleness is not something taken upon a person by one's self, but rather something that is "given" to them *by God*.

Singleness is Better in Some Situations

The apostle Paul also gives some insight into singleness.
"Yet I wish that all men were even as I myself am. However, each man has his own gift from God, one in this manner, and another in that. But I say to the unmarried and to widows that it is good for them if they remain even as I. But if they do not have self-control, let them marry; for it is better to marry than to burn.. . . I think then that this is good in view of the present distress, that it is good for a man to remain as he is. Are you bound to a wife? Do not seek to be

---

58   An underlying assumption in this text, and in all the passages referenced, is that being married includes sexual intercourse and that being single excludes it.

59   A eunuch is a man who has been castrated.

60   Matthew 19:8-9

released. Are you released from a wife? Do not seek a wife. But if you should marry, you have not sinned; and if a virgin should marry, she has not sinned. Yet such will have trouble in this life, and I am trying to spare you." 1 Corinthians 7:7-9, 26-28

The opening subject of 1 Corinthians 7 is fulfilling sexual responsibility within marriage and the important part it plays in removing the temptation for sexual sins. In this context, the assertion is made that to be single is better than to be married (1 Cor. 7:7-8). The text continues that singleness is a gift from God which not all people have been given. The mention of a "present distress" in 1 Corinthians 7:26 implies that it is easier not to be married under certain circumstances and situations than it is in others. In this instance, he was probably saying that persecution is easier to face as a single person than as a married person. Concerns about a spouse and children increase the difficulties of persecution.

<u>Singleness Enables Devotion to the Lord Without Distraction.</u>

> But I want you to be free from concern. One who is unmarried is concerned about the things of the Lord, how he may please the Lord; but one who is married is concerned about the things of the world, how he may please his wife, and {his interests} are divided. And the woman who is unmarried, and the virgin, is concerned about the things of the Lord, that she may be holy both in body and spirit; but one who is married is concerned about the things of the world, how she may please her husband. And this I say for your own benefit; not to put a restraint upon you, but to promote what is seemly, and {to secure} undistracted devotion to the Lord. (I Corinthians 7:32-35)

Such undivided devotion is noble indeed but predicated upon other previous statements. Singleness is not an option for those who "burn" with sexual desire.[61] Significantly, this "burning" is related to a lack of self-control. Self-control is the fruit of the Spirit which is the result of being filled with the Spirit. The fruit of the Spirit is not usually considered to be a special "gifted-ness" but rather the super natural consequence of allowing the Spirit of God to fill and dominate one's person.

Additionally, it is stated that to marry is not to incur sin.[62] Singleness is not something "super spiritual" which gains special merit or favor with God. Instead, singleness is one means of serving God without being distracted by other responsibilities that marriage (and children) bring.

There are indeed many "distractions" in the world. Some of them are sinful and wrong. Other "distractions" are not inherently sinful but may limit one's ability to

---

61 1 Corinthians 7:9 But if they do not have self-control, let them marry; for it is better to marry than to burn.

62 I Corinthians 7:28

serve. Marriage has the potential to be a distraction of a magnitude and duration like no other. This, of course, includes the children that are frequently the normal result of marriage. Almost all other distractions may be discarded or set aside as needed or desired to more fully serve God. One can sell, give away or abandon earthly possessions. Hobbies and pastimes can be laid aside. One can resign from a job. But marriage is a unique lifelong relationship with the associated responsibilities, cares and concerns.

Remaining single offers an opportunity for some people to direct their attention fully to serving the Lord. But it is not for everyone.

Forbidding Marriage is Condemned

Paul, in 1 Corinthians 7, commends singleness as providing greater opportunity to serve God. However, he does not forbid marrying. Indeed he states that those who marry have not sinned. On the other hand forbidding marriage is identified as one of the many legalistic practices promoted by false teachers.

> But the Spirit explicitly says that in later times some will fall away from the faith, paying attention to deceitful spirits and doctrines of demons, by means of the hypocrisy of liars seared in their own conscience as with a branding iron, {men} who forbid marriage {and advocate} abstaining from foods, which God has created to be gratefully shared in by those who believe and know the truth. For everything created by God is good, and nothing is to be rejected, if it is received with gratitude; (1 Timothy 4:1-4)

God, having created man, woman and marriage declared it to be very good. To advocate singleness as being better, or more spiritual than marriage is wrong and evidence of a false spirituality based on self-righteousness. Marriage is good. It is to be received with gratitude, and it is to be enjoyed.

Marriage contains and expresses spiritual realities about the relationship of God to His people that are found nowhere else.[63]

Some Are Instructed to Marry

As previously mentioned, those who lack self-control are instructed to marry rather than to burn with sexual passion.[64] But this is not the only instance in which marrying is to be preferred over singleness. Young widows are also told to get married to fill their lives with that which is profitable.

> Therefore, I want younger {widows} to get married, bear children, keep house, {and} give the enemy no occasion for reproach; (1 Timothy 5:14)

---

63   This concept is fully explained in the following chapters about the roles of husbands and wives.

64   I Corinthians 7:9

This instruction is given in the context of caring for widows. Younger widows were not to be cared for by the church but rather they were to get married (let their husbands care for them). Additionally, there is stated concern about their desires and their previous actions being inconsistent with remaining single. The implication is that they would fall under the admonition to marry rather than to burn.

Conclusion[65]

The gift of singleness is not simply being without a spouse. Singleness is being without the desire for a spouse, including being able to live a celibate life without distraction. Biblical singleness is more than the inability to find a suitable mate.[66] It is a special gift of God given to some people. For the Christian, the gift results in complete and wholehearted devotion to God. Singleness is not the norm but is better than the norm. Singleness is the sacrifice of human companionship for the sake of the service of God. Not all can accept this. Singleness should not be elevated above marriage and it should not be imposed externally on anyone.

---

65 The matter of a divorced person remaining single has intentionally not been addressed in this chapter. The next chapter on "Divorce" does address remarriage to some extent.

66 The chapter on finding a mate offers some suggestions for those who are having trouble in this area.

Chapter 8
Divorce: perspective on Biblical teaching

John, a 24 year old architect, stared at the stack of papers. Before him lay the documents signed by the judge. To him, those papers represented the failure of all that he had intended his relationship with Julie to be. They had been married for four short years. Then things went bad.

Although months had passed since his world collapsed upon him, he recalled the day as if it were yesterday. The note she left had rested in the same spot where the divorce papers now sat. The note read:

John,
This marriage is not going to work. I am going away for a week. When I get back, I want you out of the house. I have filed for divorce. There is someone else for me. I hope you can find someone else too. We can still be friends but we cannot continue to live this way. We make each other miserable.
*   Julie*

Several agonizing months later, not knowing where to turn, John began attending a church down the street from his home where he was encouraged to read the Bible. As he read, Jesus' teaching about marriage and divorce jumped out at him. It all seemed quite confusing so he approached the pastor and began asking questions. He had many:

- Did my divorce displease God?
- Does it make a difference that I did not want the divorce?
- Is it "OK" to divorce for any reason at all?
- Can I remarry if I find someone else? Can I remarry someone who has been divorced?
- Are there right reasons for getting a divorce?
- What if the divorce was for the wrong reasons?

Like John, many questions like these vex Christians who want to please God but are unsure what the Bible teaches about divorce. Many are already divorced. Some have been taught a particular view about divorce and embrace it without ever considering what the Bible actually says. Confusion prevails.

Even among biblically literate, sincere Christians, there is no consensus of opinion regarding divorce and the associated questions. There is no consensus on the topic among pastors. Even the most conservative Bible scholars who may agree on most

S everything else frequently don't agree about what the Bible teaches about divorce and remarriage.

Like most things, personal experience tends to significantly influence one's perspective regarding divorce. The personal emotion, trauma, grief, sadness and life changes accompanying divorce make it difficult to deal with objectively. For the divorced person who wants to be married instead of single, it is also a challenge to approach the Scripture objectively. Thus, many people unwittingly already have in their mind the answer they want before the question is asked. Consequently, when they open the Bible, they read into the Bible the answer about divorce and remarriage that they want to find.[67]

As always, it is of utmost importance to let the Word of God speak without holding to a predetermined view.

The Painful and Difficult Questions

Everyone agrees that divorce causes great pain, heartache and grief. Divorce is never easy. There are no winners. Neither spouse wins. The children never win. Neither the society nor the economy benefits from divorces. Everyone loses . . . except divorce attorneys.

The scope and focus of this chapter is intentionally narrow. It is focused on preventing the pain, heartache and "hell on earth" that often accompany divorce. It is intended primarily for those who are anticipating marriage, who have never been married, who have never been divorced, and who have never been remarried. It is an attempt to prepare God's people to succeed in marriage for God's glory. A person's perspective on divorce and remarriage before marriage will have a big impact upon whether or not the marriage will succeed.

Surrounding the issues of marriage, divorce and remarriage are many unanswered and potentially painful questions. The questions are similar to those involving a surrogate mother.

A couple, unable to have children makes an agreement with a young woman who will carry and deliver their child for them. The couple's fertilized egg is placed in the surrogate mother. All goes well for the first eight months. Then, during the ninth month the pregnant woman disappears. After an extended search, she is located but claims that the child in her womb belongs to her, not the couple.

---

67   The author's book, *Good Sermon, Brother!* analyzes this practice called "dogmatic interpretation" and provides guidelines for careful and accurate biblical interpretation. (Available at Amazon.com)

Although there is probably a legal answer to the question, the answers to the moral questions are more difficult. Whose child is it? Who does God say is the mother of the child? What is the right thing to do? . . . and . . . and . . . on and on go the questions.

The complexity of the surrogate mother situation is similar to the difficulty of the questions associated with divorce and remarriage. God's Word provides some specific teaching on parenting and on marriage but it does not provide instructions about surrogate mothers. When there is not specific teaching, often one may find that there are principles of conduct given. However, many issues are not clearly addressed by direct teaching nor even in principle. In the maze of life choices, sometimes there are not definitive answers. In the case of the surrogate mother, there is neither direct teaching nor principle. To some extent at least, by using a surrogate, the original actions were outside of God's design and instructions. After the fact, it is impossible to definitively answer some questions from God's Word. It is too late to ask some questions. Answers to many subsequent questions are not to be found. All that is left to do is to rely on God's grace.

Such is also the case with divorce and remarriage. Issues surrounding marriage are addressed by both direct teaching and by principles in the Bible. The subject of divorce is addressed by direct teaching and principle, although not as extensively as marriage. The subject of remarriage after divorce is even vaguer.

The Purpose of Discussing Divorce

As stated previously, the purpose of this chapter is to help those anticipating marriage to carefully consider how they will think biblically about divorce *BEFORE it becomes a personal issue for THEM.*

Dealing with issues before they become personal increases the ability to objectively and unemotionally consider the issue.[68] The purpose is to carefully study and understand what Scripture says on the issue before it becomes personal. For many, the issue is already personal because their parents are divorced. The purpose is not to stand in judgment of others but rather to establish a personal perspective based on an objective study of the Bible.

Divorce is painful. Needlessly raising questions without being able to offer good answers creates pain from which there is no relief. No one wants to do that. Admittedly, those reading this book who have divorce in their background will no

---

68 It seems almost impossible for someone to honestly deal with the Scripture when he is already headed down a path. The person contemplating a divorce usually finds grounds for the divorce from the pages of Scripture. In the midst of emotion and turmoil, we have trouble being honest with ourselves and with God. Because of the prevalence of divorce and remarriage, almost no one can actually be totally unaffected by the pain and emotion of divorce. This means that even more care is required to be objective.

doubt revisit some of that pain. Unanswerable questions may renew regret. There is no desire to needlessly arouse emotions.

A previously divorced or remarried person may desire to skip the remainder of this chapter. However those who plod on will benefit by being able to provide biblical teaching and counseling for those yet to cross those bridges. A humble, submissive and willing heart is required to see what God says, to admit mistakes, and to stand for truth – even though there may not be an answer to every question.

More Disclaimers

A "can of worms" is opened with any discussion of divorce and remarriage. Questions for which the Bible provides no answers will be left unanswered. The goal is to understand what God. Asking the questions that have answers now may avoid the need to later ask those questions that have no answers.

The technical aspects of the discussion is limited. Those desiring more scrutiny of a particular text have available numerous other books that address divorce and remarriage.[69] But the "vaccination" for preventing divorce does not require parsing every verb or debating the nuances of every text.[70]

Divorce is a Reality for Christians in This World

More than 50% of marriages end in divorce. Sadly, the statistics for professing Christians and unbelievers are essentially the same. Christians marry. Christians have marriage problems. Christians divorce, and Christians remarry at the same frequency as non-Christians.

Contrary to what someone might think, claiming to be a Christian does not allow anyone to escape the divorce questions. Sadly, trends in the church track closely with trends in the world. Legalized "no fault" divorce in America has resulted in the current divorce rate as if the Bible has nothing to say about it. It seems for many, legality is the bottom line of authority instead of what the Scriptures say. Similarly, the teaching about divorce from the pulpit has tracked with the culture. Many churches just do not teach on marriage, divorce and remarriage because it can be offensive and will possibly turn people away.

Many factors contribute to the likelihood of a married person contemplating divorce. Two selfish human beings cannot exist together for days, weeks, months

---

69   For example, The Family by John MacArthur, Jr. includes an overview of the issues. Divorce by John Murray gives a detailed and exegetical analysis of relevant texts.

70   Much of the technical analysis of the texts dealing with divorce is motivated by a desire to justify either what has already happened or what one desires to happen. Too often these texts are approached with preconceived ideas and are interpreted in ways to make them say what the reader want them to say.

and years on end without rubbing each other the wrong way. In marriage, the opportunities to butt heads are as numerous as the seconds in the day. When conflict arises and seems like a "no-win" situation it is common to contemplate divorce as a possible solution. The prevalence, and widespread acceptance of divorce contributes greatly to divorce being considered as a viable option when things get difficult.

An Ounce of Prevention is Better . . .

Like with dating, the best time to ask and settle questions about divorce is before one needs too. The circumstances that lead to contemplating divorce also put emotions on a world class roller coaster. It is impossible to objectively study and understand the Bible in the midst of emotional turmoil. The time to consider what God has to say about marriage, divorce and remarriage is before it is personal and before it is emotional. Emotions and the heat of the battle often send people to the Bible to find permission to do what they have already decided to do. It would be very unlikely that a person contemplating divorce would be able to objectively evaluate what God says about divorce when their situation requires it.

Contemplating divorce is like engaging in hand-to-hand combat on the front lines. It is extremely difficult to learn how to clean and inspect a rifle when embroiled in battle. The heat of the battle requires that the rifle be continually fired regardless of its condition. Emotions, like a runaway freight train, push for self-protection, self-preservation and revenge. When this happens, there is neither time, desire nor ability to calmly sit down and objectively consider what God says.

Ideally, God's children would always be eager to seek His perspective. In reality though, after the battle lines are drawn, it is rare for someone to say, "Let's just sit down and see what God has to say about all this." Hurt feelings, agitated emotions, long term strife and wounded pride all get in the way. If either party suggests seeking counsel, suspicion and accusations that the counselor will be biased often prevail. Once embroiled in conflict, it is very difficult to objectively search for the truth.

The time to answer all the divorce questions is before they become personal. This chapter raises questions, encourages contemplation, and urges adopting a biblical position on divorce before the wedding day, preferably even before dating begins.

Pastors can help by requiring marriage candidates to study and verbalize their views on divorce prior to marriage. This might save some marriages and possibly even prevent some weddings from actually happening.[71]

---

71 Recognizing the importance of premarital counseling, some states are passing laws that people marrying be given the option to have a "no-fault" marriage, or a covenant marriage, which would be much harder to dissolve. This is kind of a prenuptial non divorce agreement.

Divorce, as it Relates to the Definition of Marriage

Embracing a biblical definition of marriage has significant implications for how one views divorce. Marriage was defined as:

> a lifelong, divinely instituted, committed relationship between a man and a woman resulting in the two becoming one.

According to Jesus, the joining together in marriage is an act of God, which man is not to break.[72] Significantly, Jesus' assertion was given in a discussion about divorce. Jesus' answer should have been the end of the discussion. But then, as now, people did not like what Jesus said for various reasons. When asked about divorce, Jesus went back to the definition of marriage.

According to the biblical definition of marriage:

- Divorce is the dissolving of a divine, God-ordained institution.
- Divorce is breaking a commitment for life, before the life is over.
- Divorce is ripping apart the two who God joined into one.
- Divorce is the dividing of a physical, emotional and spiritual union.

It is difficult to reconcile divorce with the definition of marriage. Attempting to reconcile them raises many questions, most of which do not have easy answers, if they have answers at all.

These unanswerable questions suggest that either the definition of marriage is wrong or that divorce is inconsistent with the definition of marriage. (There may be much profit for the reader to ponder and reach some conclusions about this before continuing.)

Additional Needed Considerations

It would be wonderful if Christians simply adopted a biblical definition of marriage. Divorce would be viewed as inconsistent with the nature of marriage. They would be fully committed to remain married and not divorce.[73]

Unfortunately, the issue of divorce is not so easily dismissed for a number of reasons:

---

72 Matthew 19:6 Consequently they are no longer two, but one flesh. What therefore God has joined together, let no man separate.

73 In the not too distant past, all marriage vows included "till death do us part" because people understood the permanent nature of marriage as described in the Bible. Although the vows are still often said, they are often not embraced as more than cheap words.

- The Bible does speak about the existence of divorce and gives some regulations associated with divorce. These passages need to be understood fully in their context.
- There are many, including conservative Christians, who allow for divorce in a variety of circumstances. These reference the Bible to support their position. The reasons and basis for the different positions need to be understood.
- There is wide variation in the views about divorce and they all cannot be right.
- A large percentage of people are divorced. Questions about remarriage will be answered differently depending upon one's understanding of divorce.

For these reasons it is necessary to consider the various views that are held. Most important is honestly and objectively understanding what the Bible says about divorce and remarriage.

The Power of Starting Points

There are three very important factors that tend to greatly influence the conclusions people reach when studying what the Bible says about divorce. These factors are interrelated. The factors can be stated as questions and include:

- What is the degree of personal involvement? Although great effort may be exerted to be objective, everyone is influenced by experiences. Personal history and the experiences of others frequently influence one's conclusions regarding what the Bible teaches about divorce and remarriage. The prevalence of divorce and remarriage subjectively causes rejection of some fairly clear biblical teachings as "unpractical."

- What questions are asked? Presuppositions are often revealed in the way questions about divorce are stated. Very few come to the Word of God asking, "What does God say?" Instead, answers to specific questions are often sought such as, "Does God allow divorce?" "Under what circumstances does God allow divorce?" "What are legitimate grounds for divorce?" "Can I remarry after I divorce?" The questions being asked reveal the assumptions. Assumptions influence the conclusions.

- What texts are selected as primary? People tend to pick one passage in the Bible as the primary text on divorce. Other texts become subordinate to the primary text. Seemingly contradictory passages are "forced" to conform to the "primary" one. The passage selected as primary often depends on the assumptions held and the corresponding questions being asked.

These factors are biases that are frequently unrecognized by the person who holds them. Selection of a particular text as "primary" and the questions asked reflect one's assumptions and will significantly influence the conclusions. In other words, one tends to read these factors into the Bible and find the answer that one wants to find. Instead, honest biblical interpretation is humble and carefully seeks to learn what God says so that it can be obeyed.

It is common for the conclusions reached regarding what the Bible says about divorce to depend largely on one's starting point.[74] Recognizing potential biases will increase the possibility of reaching an objective conclusion.

Starting Points

Consider how asking each of the following questions as a starting point may skew the results of studying the Bible to determine what it says about divorce:

- What is marriage?
- Does God approve of divorce?
- Is it ever acceptable to get a divorce?
- When is it acceptable to get a divorce?
- For what reasons can I get a divorce and then get remarried?
- If I divorce for good reasons, can I remarry?
- If I divorce for wrong reasons, can I still remarry?

Obviously, differing motives and presuppositions are behind each question. To some extent, the question becomes a self-fulfilling prophecy. The answer is almost predetermined by choosing which question to ask.

Additionally, the question that is asked will determine what Bible text will be considered primary. A person who asks "What is marriage?" will most likely begin with a different passage and come to a different conclusion than one who asks, "When is it acceptable to get a divorce?" The motivation behind asking the questions are different. The motivation behind the question will also likely influence the way any particular passage is interpreted.

Individual Accountability

There is a wide divergence of opinions held by godly men of faith about divorce and remarriage. This highlights the importance that each individual be sure in their own mind that they are doing the right thing. As with all biblical teaching, God will hold every individual accountable for their understanding, as well as for their

---

74 Not all the answers can be right. Each Bible passage has only one correct interpretation. Thus when people assert different interpretations for the same passage, one or all of them are wrong. Principles of interpretation must be followed to correctly interpret the Bible. Faulty interpretation underlies much of the confusion about what the Bible says about divorce; ibid: *Good Sermon, Brother!*

actions. To lazily say that, "so and so taught me this, therefore I am to be excused" will not be acceptable to God. Indeed, the teacher will be responsible for what they have taught, but individuals retain their personal responsibility for knowing what the Word of God says and obeying it themselves.

Because of the variations in positions among sincere and genuine Christian scholars, the principles found in Romans 14 may be applicable.[75] Therefore, "let each one be fully convinced in his own mind." This text focuses on individual matters that must be held as a personal conviction. Also it says "whatever is not of faith is sin." Where there is doubt there is sin. If one is not completely confident, then it is sinful to do it. Each one is to be fully and totally convinced that what they are doing is approved by God, otherwise it is sin. This is true of all areas of life, all decision and all actions. Without faith it is impossible to please God.[76] This cannot be used as an excuse to do whatever one may choose. Each one is accountable to God to know and to obey what He has said.

What Does the Bible Say About Divorce?

The following chart identifies the passages most frequently cited as pertaining directly to divorce and remarriage. The left column lists biblical texts and summarizes their content, purpose and context. The right column offers observations about the text that are significant to properly understanding and applying the text.[77] The context of each passage is of utmost importance. For it has been rightfully said that "a text without a context is a pretext." This means that if a text is taken out of context then it can be distorted to say something different than what God intended. Unfortunately, in the discussion of divorce and remarriage, taking verses out of context is common.

Text Related to Divorce – Questions, Context, and Purpose	Answers, Conclusions and Observations
Genesis 2:18-25 – Defines marriage, and describes the origin of marriage. God instituted marriage; Man and woman become one flesh in marriage.	The two are no longer two, they are one, united to one another.

---

75 Romans 14:5 and 23; The author personally does not consider the issue of divorce and remarriage to be unclear in the scriptures. However, because of widely divergent positions held by other very godly men, the author teaches the Bible, and deals with others as if it is a Romans 14 type of issue.

76 Hebrews 11:6

77 The conclusions offered represent the author's understanding. Since a full exegetical analysis of each text is not the intent, the big picture is presented as a practical basis for considering all the passages in one place.

Text Related to Divorce – Questions, Context, and Purpose	Answers, Conclusions and Observations
Deuteronomy 24:1-4 Can a person who is divorced,remarry their previous spouse if they have remarried and divorced in the meantime? Ensured that women who were divorced would be freed by a certification of the divorce. Prohibits remarriage of a former wife after she has been married to a second man.	This law is related to God's covenant with Israel; It is not directly applicable to Gentiles or Christians. The answer to the question is "No, the divorced and remarried woman may not return to her first husband." Divorce is not commanded, but regulated. Possible Application: Do not remarry your previous wife if she has remarried after divorcing you.
Ezra 9-10 Israel incurred guilt by intermarrying with nations around them which was forbidden by God. The Israelites confessed their sin. Ezra said God required the Israelites to put away their foreign wives and they did. (divorced and left?)	Israelite men *divorced (?)* their foreign wives in order to establish a proper relationship with God. This action was related to Israel as a nation. God prohibited intermarriage to hinder being influenced into idolatry. Exactly how this text may apply to questions about Christian's divorcing is unclear. Application of this text may relate to personal holiness and separation from sinful influences in the world. For example, polygamous situations may have application.
Nehemiah 13:23-31 Seems to imply that Nehemiah, like Ezra, required the putting away of foreign wives.	See the discussion above about the text in Ezra. The two situations are similar and may apply in similar ways. As with the Ezra text, application is uncertain.
Malachi 3:14-16 God hates divorce. Divorce is dealing treacherously with one's wife. Divorce was part of the reason that God brought the curses upon Israel andJudah.	Divorce is listed among those things that greatly displease God. This seems to indicate God's great displeasure with those who break the vows made in marriage.

Text Related to Divorce – Questions, Context, and Purpose	Answers, Conclusions and Observations
Matthew 5:27-32 see also Luke 16:18 When is a person guilty of committing adultery? The topic of the text is adultery and the matter of divorce and remarriage is just one instance in which adultery occurs.	In the Sermon on the Mount, Jesus was establishing the universal failure of everyone to keep God's law. Jesus emphasizes that sin includes violation of the law, as well as sinful thoughts and heart motives.
Guilt for adultery occurs when: *One thinks it in their mind, or *One divorces his wife, or *One who is divorced is married to another. The clause, "except for fornication" is often called "the exception clause." The exception places guilt for adultery associated with the divorce on the previously unfaithful spouse. In the absence of prior adultery, the party who divorces is guilty of adultery.	He said that divorcing one's spouse makes them responsible for the adultery of their spouse. (The assumption seems to be that they remarry and commit adultery.) In the case of prior adultery, the unfaithful one was already guilty of adultery and therefore the divorce is not the cause of their adultery. Marrying a divorced person is committing adultery.

Text Related to Divorce – Questions, Context, and Purpose	Answers, Conclusions and Observations
Matthew 19:3-13 see also Mark 10:1-12 Is it lawful to divorce for any cause at all? (i.e. at any whim.)	Divorce, for any reason, is not desired by God because it violates God's design for marriage.
Jesus answered: "No!" & explains referring to Genesis where marriage was establishment and is defined:	Jesus' answer was a simple "no" to the basic question of whether a person can divorce for any reason at all.
*The two have become one flesh. *God has joined them together. *Let not man separate them.	Marriage is an act of God. Divorce is an act of man.
Jesus then answered why Moses gave instructions about divorce: Divorce was allowed because of hardness of heart. Divorce was not intended from the beginning.	God never commanded people to get divorced but the people thought He had. Divorce is an act of a hard heart. Divorce was not part of God's design or intent.
Whoever divorces commits adultery (This passage also includes the "except for immorality" clause as in Matthew 5.)	Adultery is involved in divorce.
He who marries a divorced woman commits adultery.	Adultery is involved in remarriage of a divorced person.
Based on this teaching, the disciples concluded that it was better not to marry.	

Text Related to Divorce – Questions, Context, and Purpose	Answers, Conclusions and Observations
Romans 7:1-6 What is the Christian's relationship to the Old Testament law?	Attempting to keep the law after becoming a Christian is like an adulterous relationship. You cannot be "married to" Christ and the law at the same time.
This passage uses the bonds of marriage as an <u>illustration</u> of the relationship of the Christian to the law. The illustration says:	While it is not the main point of the text, the illustration is based on the fact that adultery occurs when one's spouse is living and one is married to another person.
Law applies while a person lives.	
As long as the husband lives, the wife is bound to him.	
If, while her husband lives she is bound to another man, she is called adulterous.	
If the husband dies, she may be bound to another man without being adulterous.	
The point of the text is that because the Christian has died to the law, he is joined legitimately to Christ and is no longer bound to the law.	

Text Related to Divorce – Questions, Context, and Purpose	Answers, Conclusions and Observations
1 Corinthians 7:1-28,39 What are the duties of the married and what is best for singles? This passage begins with a discussion of the sexual responsibilities of spouses.	Each spouse is responsible to meet the physical needs of the other.
Regarding divorce: The wife should not leave her husband. 7:10	Neither a believing husband or wife should leave their spouse, even if the other spouse is unbelieving.
Two options for the wife that leaves her husband. 7:11 1) remain unmarried (sexually inactive), or 2) be reconciled	If a spouse leaves, they have two options, remain single or be reunited.
The husband should not send his wife away. 7:11	
Live with an unbelieving spouse and do not leave them. (7:12-16)	
If the unbelieving spouse leaves the spouse is not bound to fulfill conjugal responsibility. 7:15 (see verses 7:1-5)	When one's spouse leaves them, they are not bound to meet the sexual needs of the partner who left.
If one marries they do not sin (close proximity to "are you loosed from a wife") 7:27-28	
Marriage is binding until the death of one spouse. After one's spouse dies, they one may remarry in the Lord. 7:39	Death of a spouse is legitimate grounds for remarriage.
1 Timothy 4:3 What are some of the teachings of false teachers? False teachers forbid marriage.	Marriage is good. It is not to be rejected; but is to be received with gratitude. It is sanctified by Word of God and prayer.

A survey of these texts mentioning or relating to divorce paint a clear picture that marriage is the norm, and it is good. Divorce is the exception and is associated with sin. It seems obvious that God's will is that people get married and not get divorced. Most everyone agrees that God's moral will and desire are that after someone is married, they are to remain married.

But . . . because over 50% of marriages end in divorce . . . and because churches are filled with people who have been previously divorced . . . it is necessary to consider the questions of divorce and remarriage more extensively.

The disciples seemed to well understand the gravity of divorce from what Jesus said in Matthew 19. They concluded that because 1) divorce was not part of God's plan, 2) divorce arises from a hard heart and 3) the one who divorces commits adultery and makes their spouse commit adultery it is better not to marry.[78]

Part of the reason that divorce and remarriage are such significant and controversial issues in the Christian church today is because they are so prevalent. Those who have divorced and those who are contemplating divorce want to be justified in their own eyes, in the eyes of others and in the eyes of God. Many people simply adopt a view of divorce and remarriage that justifies their actions. However, determining God's view on any subject should begin with what God says, not with looking for self- justification.

Why So Many Views on Divorce?

Most of the positions held regarding divorce and remarriage appeal to one or more of the passages included in the above chart. The variation in position can largely be attributed to the differences in 1) the text selected as being primary and 2) the starting questions which are asked. Both of these reveal assumptions and perspectives in approaching the texts.

Below is a summary of the prevailing views on divorce today. The summary includes a title, an assessment of the view, and a list of the results of embracing the view.

Common Views on Divorce

#1 "Popular View" Divorce and subsequent remarriage is allowed for any reason.

This view is represented by current laws regarding no fault divorce. This view begins outside of the Bible, disregards the authority of Scripture and is devoid of faith. This is not a prevalent view among Christians.

Personal happiness and self-fulfillment are considered most important. Morality is considered to be personal and subjective. Any divorce or remarriage (or any other relationship) is considered acceptable if the person feels that it brings personal happiness.

---

78 Matthew 19:1-10 Discussion of the "exception clause" follow under Common Views of Divorce.

Although happiness is the goal of this view, most divorces result in life long struggles and happiness remains elusive.

#2 "Reasonable Position" or "Position of Compassion"

Divorce (and remarriage) is considered permissible if one or more of the following exist within the marriage:

1. Adultery.
2. Desertion by spouse.
3. Physical abuse of spouse or child.
4. Mental abuse of spouse or child.
5. numerous other reasons if Scripture is handled loosely.

This view asks the question: Under what conditions does God allow divorce and remarriage?

The answer to the question is found in Matthew 5 and 19 that include the "exception clause" to allow for divorce and remarriage in cases of spouse's sexual immorality. Additionally 1 Corinthians 7:15 "not under bondage" clause is considered to indicate that desertion by a spouse is grounds for divorce and remarriage. Other Bible passages that do not directly discuss divorce may be used to justify abuse as a basis for divorce.

This view considers that the divorce was acceptable or "legitimate" based on some certain criteria, and remarriage is considered acceptable also.

Part of the motivation for this view is the desire to have compassion on those who have made mistakes in their relationships. It is considered too hard and harsh to say that a person must either reconcile to their spouse or remain single. Compassion trumps all else in this view.

#3 "Prior to Conversion" Divorce

This view says if the divorce happened prior to becoming a Christian then it does not matter what the reasons or the circumstances were. (This view may also include or exclude aspects of view #2 described above.)

This view is based on 2 Corinthians 5:17, which says, "Therefore, if any man is in Christ, he is a new creature; the old things passed away; behold, new things have come."

According to this view, when a person becomes a Christian they start with a new slate and what happened before their salvation is a non-issue, including divorce and remarriage.

#4 "Limited Divorce, No Remarriage"

This view allows for divorce in cases of hardness, unrepentance unfaithfulness, desertion, etc., but does not allow for remarriage in any instance, regardless of the circumstances.

This view typically asks "What is marriage?" or "Can the marriage bond be broken?" or "What breaks the marriage bond?"

Genesis 2:24 and Matthew 19:1-12 are viewed as primary texts defining marriage. These passages state that marriage is a lifetime bond established by God that cannot be broken.

Considers that the "exception clause" of Matthew 5:32 and 19:9 to apply to the questions being asked and answered in the context. The "except" in Matthew 5:32 does not allow for divorce, but only shifts blame for who is responsible for the adultery as a result of divorce. The "not under bondage" in 1 Corinthians 7 applies not to the marriage bond, but to the moral bond and requirement in the context to meet the spouse's sexual needs. The statements that the marriage bond remains until the death of one spouse in Romans 7 and 1 Corinthians 7:39 are held to mean that the marriage cannot be broken before God apart from the death of one partner.

Any sexual relationship outside the original marriage relationship while the original spouse lives is considered adulterous.

Considers it best that there never be divorce.

Being divorced by an unbelieving spouse relieves the believer of marital obligations, but it does not free them from the marriage.

Holds that it is not necessarily wrong for a Christian to obtain a divorce from an unbelieving, deserting or unfaithful spouse; however the grounds for divorce are not considered to be legitimate grounds for remarriage.

The only options for a divorced Christian are to be reconciled to the estranged spouse or to remain single as stated in 1 Corinthians 7:11

Death of spouse is the only thing considered to break the marriage bond and is therefore the only basis for remarriage. 1 Corinthians 7:39 and Romans 7:1-6

#5 "No Divorce, No Remarriage"

Does not allow for divorce or remarriage in any instance. It is like view #4, but considers all divorces and as well as all remarriages to be immoral. May even not allow remarriage after the death of a spouse.

The above chart summarizing the biblical texts dealing with divorce and the various views regarding divorce provide an introduction to the divorce and remarriage issues. Familiarity with these texts and views will enable further and more detailed study of the various passages and views.

A License to Divorce

One's view on divorce and remarriage changes the odds for the success or failure of their marriage. This fact is often overlooked. The person who enters marriage believing that nothing but death will end the marriage will be cautious about who they marry. They will find a way to make the marriage work. Their attitude and effort will be different from the one who thinks that divorce and remarriage are among their acceptable choices. Consequently, it would be wise to carefully consider how you and your potential future spouse view divorce before getting married. To think that it is easy to walk away from a marriage means that it is more likely to happen.

The discussion here is intended to help those yet anticipating marriage. Adopting a biblical view of marriage and divorce increases the likelihood that a marriage will endure and be pleasant – thereby "Avoiding Hell on Earth!" What you and the person you marry believe about divorce will have an impact on how much work goes into dating and marriage before throwing in the towel.

The Author's Perspective

The author embraces view #4, as stated above, considering it to be the most consistent with what the Bible teaches. This view does not answer every question. However, it seems to best represent the teaching of the whole of Scripture. It is the view that seems to be most consistent with the definition of marriage. It seems to best represent the heart of God. The beginning question in this discussion should be, "What is marriage?" Genesis chapters one and two are foundational because Jesus answered questions about divorce by quoting from Genesis.[79] These texts describe marriage prior to sin. In salvation the Christian has the power of God to overcome sin and to be partially restored to what marriage was like before the fall.

The main criticisms of view #4 are that it is unpractical and lacking compassion for those who are divorced or remarried. Although these criticisms may have validity in some instances, this does not undermine the position as unbiblical. View #4 is only unpractical for those who have gone beyond that which is best, that which is specified in Scripture. As for compassion, to teach God's high view of marriage and God's low view of divorce may enable those yet to marry and those still married to approach marriage in a way that will promote God's best.

---

79   In Matthew 19:5-6, Jesus quotes from Genesis 1:27 and Genesis 2:24 in the same breath.

That is very compassionate. There is grief and compassion for those who have experienced the pain and agony of divorce, but Scripture must not be compromised to accommodate the masses.

Significantly, among those who hold any but the first view, almost everyone agrees that God's best excludes divorce. So, choosing to date or marry someone who is adverse to divorce is a better starting point than choosing someone who is willing to consider divorce as an option.

Other Biblical Considerations Regarding Divorce

In addition to the direct and indirect teachings of Scripture on divorce and remarriage there are other things to be considered. A committed Christian should carefully consider spiritual truths and principles from the whole of the Scriptures. They should not limit their understanding of divorce to the passages usually associated with divorce.

Christians are Not Allowed to Sue Another Christian

If two married people are Christians, they cannot obtain a legal divorce without disobeying 1 Corinthians 6:1-11.

This text prohibits one Christian from suing another Christian in the civil courts. Instead, disputes among Christians are to be settled within the church. So, if both spouses are Christians, divorce is not allowed. The church should settle the marital dispute. However, if either spouse is unwilling to submit to the church, then church discipline should follow.[80] If one, or both spouses are considered to be unbelievers by means of church discipline, then civil action may be an option. However, two Christians who divorce are violating this clear teaching.

Most Divorces Include the Sin of Not Forgiving

It is apparent that underlying almost all divorces is a lack of forgiveness. The separation that occurs in a divorce is related to the sin of at least one spouse and the unwillingness to forgive. Frequently there is the sin of both and the unwillingness of both to forgive.

The Bible requires that Christians forgive as God has forgiven them. Ephesians 4:32 requires:

> Be kind to one another, tender-hearted, forgiving each other, just as God in Christ also has forgiven you.

---

80 Matthew 18:15ff and Galatians 61ff explain the process of church discipline that seeks to confront sin for the sake of repentance and restoration of relationships. This includes unlimited forgiveness.

There may be reasons and circumstances that a person could forgive and yet still divorce, but in most instances the divorcing person is not willing to forgive. Many people think they have forgiven, but they simply do not understand what forgiveness is. Forgiveness is relieving the other person of any obligation or debt incurred as a result of an offense or sin. The person who forgives takes the debt upon himself and relieves the other person of the debt. Forgiveness does not mean it is forgotten, but that the debt is gone and will not be held against the other person.

Additionally, according to Scripture, failing to forgive someone's sin is an indication of either a lack of receipt of God's forgiveness or, at least, the lack of appreciation for it.

Matthew 6:14-15 "For if you forgive others for their transgressions, your heavenly Father will also forgive you. But if you do not forgive others, then your Father will not forgive your transgressions.

And, in response to Peter's question about the number of times a person was to forgive, Jesus told a parable about one who refused to forgive. At the conclusion of the parable He said, My heavenly Father will also turn you over to the tormentors, if each of you does not forgive his brother from your heart.[81]

If there is such a thing as a legitimate divorce, it must include forgiveness. No matter what other issues exist, if the person initiating the divorce is doing so because they have not forgiven, then the divorce is wrong.

Adultery is NOT the Divorce Trump Card

Every list of supposedly legitimate reasons for divorce includes adultery. It is not surprising that adultery usually tops the list, and for good reason. Marital unfaithfulness is considered a grave sin by most. It is viewed as the most basic breach of the marriage contract. Sexual impurity (adultery) is also in the "exception clauses" most often referenced as biblical grounds for divorce:

> but I say to you that everyone who divorces his wife, except for the reason of unchastity (fornication), makes her commit adultery; and whoever marries a divorced woman commits adultery. (Matthew 5:32)

> And I say to you, whoever divorces his wife, except for immorality, and marries another woman commits adultery. (Matthew 19:9)

However, careful study of these passages in their contexts reveals the emphasis is not so focused on the "exception" clauses as it is often made to appear. The focus

---

81 Matthew 18:21-35

on the exception clause arises from efforts to find acceptable reasons for divorce instead of trying to understand the broad point the text is making.

Matthew 5 is part of the Sermon on the Mount which teaches that no one is righteous enough to enter the kingdom of heaven. In this sermon, Jesus uses the issue of adultery (5:27-32) as an example to prove the point that no one is righteous. He says the following people are guilty of adultery:

- 5:27 - the one who commits the physical act of adultery
- 5:28-30 - the one who commits adultery in their heart/mind
- 5:31-32 - the one who divorces his wife makes her commit adultery.
- 5:31-32 - the one who marries a divorced woman commits adultery

So, who is not guilty of adultery?

Jesus is not saying when one can divorce, but that no one is righteous because, although they may not have physically committed adultery, in their hearts they are just as guilty as everyone else. Jesus identifies adultery as a heart issue and shows that everyone is guilty of adultery.

To apply Jesus' teaching in this context honestly and without prejudice has significant implications for the divorce discussion. If adultery is a legitimate cause for divorce, and all men have committed adultery in their heart, then every wife would have God-sanctioned grounds for divorcing her husband. There is an inherent weakness and inconsistency in supporting divorce from this text.

The exception clause in Matthew 5:31-32 only shifts the guilt for the adultery that results from a divorce. The exception allows that if a woman is already committing adultery and her husband divorces her, then he is not making her commit adultery – she already is adulterous.

Similarly, the text in Matthew 19 is often dealt with loosely without giving appropriate consideration to the context. The text is often approached looking for a legitimate reason to divorce rather than allowing the text to speak for itself. A little attention to the details of the text reveals that the exception clause is not intended to provide a license to divorce.

Question (Pharisees): Is it lawful for a man to divorce his wife for any reason at all? (Matthew 19:3)

Answer (Jesus): [No!] "have you not read that he who created them from the beginning made them male and female, and said, "for this reason a man shall leave his father and mother and be joined to his wife, and the two shall become one flesh?" so they are no longer two, but one flesh. What therefore God has joined together, let no man separate. (Matthew 19:4-6)

Question (Pharisees): why then did Moses command to give her a certificate of divorce and send her away?

Answer (Jesus): Because of your hardness of heart [Moses permitted you to divorce your wives; but from the beginning it has not been this way.]

Elaboration (Jesus): And I say to you, whoever divorces his wife, except for immorality, and marries another woman commits adultery.

Jesus says:

- Divorce is not allowed for any reason at all.
- Divorce certificates were allowed because of their hard hearts.
- Divorce and remarriage typically results in adultery.

The exception clause is indeterminate in this context. The parallel passages in Mark 10:2ff and Luke 16:18 omit the exception clause altogether. However, the point of the text is clear.

To make adultery the divorce trump card, as is often used, ignores the purpose of these texts and ignores the context. Everyone is guilty of adultery. Adultery can, and should be, forgiven. But adultery does not provide a license to divorce like many people are often led to think.[82]

Divorce Unveiled

Most divorces happen because people are selfish, sinful and simply refuse to do what is necessary to make the marriage work. Usually the decision to divorce is made first, and biblical support of the decision is sought afterward. Seldom are divorces actually based on the reasons put forth. Most divorces are actually based on the "I deserve happiness" philosophy, even when other reasons exist or are stated.

Even when there are supposedly legitimate grounds for divorce, there are numerous and significant biblical truths that would stop true Christians from divorcing in most cases. God's design for marriage, resolving issues in the church instead of civil courts, and the requirement for forgiveness all stand in the way of a Christian divorcing their Christian spouse.

Conclusion and Encouragement

Everyone agrees that divorce is never God's best. How one views divorce changes the nature of their marriage. The one who thinks divorce is okay will be okay with thinking about divorcing. The one who shuns the idea of divorce as an option will devote the time and energy necessary to get through the hard times without

---

82 Adultery is a grievous sin that causes great harm to marriages. Marital unfaithfulness is a breach of trust that has significant consequences. Forgiveness, much effort ,and a period of time is usually required to restore trust within the relationship.

contemplating divorce as an option thus, divorce will be much less likely to happen.

Viewpoints on divorce are available to support every possible divorce and remarriage scenario. People who want to justify themselves will find a view to fit their situation and alleviate them of any guilt. But those who want to please God will base their decisions on what God says, rather than on their own desires. This is what Galatians 5:17 says, "For the flesh sets its desire against the Spirit, and the Spirit against the flesh; for these are in opposition to one another, so that you may not do the things that you please." The question for the follower of Jesus is "What does the Spirit desire?"

It is not the primary intent of this book to convince any person that one view about divorce is right and all others are wrong. The intent is to encourage individuals reading this book to carefully and seriously consider the Scriptures on divorce and remarriage **before** they enter into a marriage relationship. Be fully convinced of what God says and be totally obedient to that.

As previously stated, there are many unanswerable questions that will arise for a person who is divorced. More questions exist for those who are remarried. The best way to resolve those questions personally is to never get into the situation. An unwavering commitment to the marriage and to God to make it work no matter what comes is needed. If marriage is entered with the perspective that divorce is not an option then it is amazing how much harder one will work at "making it work."

A Word about Crossed Bridges

For those who have already crossed the divorce and/or remarriage bridges, seek to please God from this point forward. Learn and implement the principles found in God's Word wherever you are now. Leave those unanswered questions at the foot of the cross where sins are forgiven, mercy is applied and God's great grace abounds. Confess your past sins as God makes them known. Praise God for His grace and make it your purpose and intent to be faithful to Him from this point forward.

Have compassion on those who have not crossed the bridges you have, confess your sins to them. Hold up God's standard for them and encourage them to make choices that are pleasing to God. Please do not justify your past actions contrary to Scripture and become a stumbling block for others.

Among the many causes for difficulty in marriages, and often underlying divorces, is ineffective communication between spouses. Problems escalate because misunderstandings hinder effective communication. The next chapter offers some help in understanding the need to effectively communicate and how to do it.

Chapter 9
Communication: To Speak or Not to Speak

I thought that you thought that we both thought what I thought but now I think that you think that I think differently, and I am not so sure.

<u>A True Story</u>

The tension was thick as the family drove down the road. Husband, wife and children alike knew that there was some problem. Yet no individual had enough pieces of the puzzle to identify the source of the tension. Seeds of the problem were sowed the evening before when the wife had asked her husband, "What time do you want to leave in the morning?" He replied, "After breakfast."

Breakfast was habitually at 7 a.m. The alarm went off as normal. Husband and wife set to their normal routine. The wife exercised while the husband showered and read his Bible. While the wife showered and prepared breakfast, the husband went out of doors to stoke a brush pile fire, exercising care to ensure he returned to the house in advance of the morning meal time.

At breakfast, tension filled the air as the husband and wife spoke to each other with short, guarded and choppy exchanges. What would have normally been routine instructions to children were spouted with impatience and frustration. Finally everyone was in the car. The family was on the road to a conference more than an hour away. They would be late for the start of the first session.

After some minutes in the car, one spouse said, "Are we going to be like this all day?"

That question opened the door for a conversation that revealed the source of the tension and eventually put it to rest. There had been poor communication. There was some misunderstanding resulting in the husband and wife having very different expectations about the start to their day. Different expectations were not the problem. The problem was that both failed to realize that the other one had a different expectation. Thus tension ensued. Although understanding had been sought and attempted, a common understanding had not been reached. Consider how the different expectations came to exist:

<u>Wife:</u> The wife had inquired early about the desired departure time. She wanted to please her husband. She wanted to be able to ensure the family would be on the road at the time her husband desired. To her "after breakfast" meant <u>immediately</u> after breakfast, at 7:30. She had good reason to reach this conclusion. This departure time would ensure arrival at the conference in time

for the start of the first session at 9:00 am. She knew her husband was always prompt and considered it rude for someone to be late. When the husband went outside rather than helping ready the children for the day, it was viewed as inconsiderate and became a source of irritation. "How could he ask me to leave "after breakfast" and then do nothing to make that possible?" She had expected that he would help by getting the children dressed and ready to go while she prepared breakfast. This of course did not happen; thus frustration and tension was created between them.

Husband: When the husband said "after breakfast" he intended that the family would leave when ready, at some unspecified time after breakfast. He anticipated that it would be hectic getting everyone ready to go at a particular point in time. He decided it was not worth the trouble to get the whole family to the conference for the start of the first session. Thus, to lighten the burden on his wife and family, he left the departure time somewhat vague and open ended. At least that was his intent. "After breakfast" was intended to allow flexibility to minimize stress and pressure on everyone, especially his wife. The husband assumed that they both understood, "We will get to the conference, when we get to the conference. It is okay if we are a little late this time." Therefore he felt free to poke at the fire a few minutes. Sensing the tension when he came back inside left him scratching his head.

Fortunately, the subsequent discussion in the car cleared the air of misunderstanding and reestablished a harmonious marriage relationship. Frequently though, the resolution of such a minor problem does not quickly occur. Often, what begins as a slight miscommunication is never resolved and eventually combine with other irritations to contribute to complex and confusing marital strife that is almost impossible to sort out.

Inadequate communication is a major source of marital stress, disharmony and conflict. Almost every discussion about what is needed for a successful marriage includes the importance of good communication. Volumes are devoted to effective communication, especially within marriage. This chapter intends primarily to raise awareness of the problem, to introduce the basics of communication and to encourage further study.

Familiarity Hampers Communication

Complacency is one major contributor to communication failures. Familiarity breeds complacency. Typically, the more familiar one is with another person, the less effort will be exerted to communicate clearly. Fortunately, communication is usually successful even when it is vague, incomplete, imprecise or sloppy. Unfortunately, though, this ability to "usually succeed" in communication sets the stage for significant failures in communication as well. Since no special effort is required most of the time, a loose and casual attitude develops toward communication. That casualness sometimes leads to communication failures.

Fortunately, most communication failures, although perhaps annoying or humorous, are relatively insignificant. Unfortunately though, sometimes a miscommunication creates significant problems. Occasionally, the problems are irreversibly damaging in a relationship.

In marriage, the frequency and familiarity factors of communication are compounded. There are many occasions for sharing information with the same person day after day, year after year. Knowledge about one's spouse and how they communicate become the basis for assumptions. The assumptions are usually correct. But when the assumptions are wrong, the problems occur.

<u>Understanding Effective Communication</u>

Communication is often given little conscious thought. It is automatic. It is a habit. Most people have a thought, speak their mind and expect others to understand. Few actually ponder the complexity of communication and make a conscious effort to ensure it is done well. Although communication "just happens," **effective** communication takes purposeful effort. Effective communication doesn't "just happen."

The responsibility to ensure that communication is effective is often wrongly thought to lie solely with the speaker. Instead, ensuring effective communication is the responsibility of <u>both</u> parties. Each person should assume 100% of the responsibility for the effectiveness of the communication. Communication will be more complete, accurate and effective when both parties accept responsibility for the transaction.

<u>Defining Communication</u>

Communication. What is it? Communication is not one person talking and another person listening. For example, a math teacher can be talking fervently and a student listening intently with no communication occurring. In contrast, a mother may scowl at her five year old boy tracking mud across the kitchen floor, - a look that communicates very well. Communication is not about words. Communication is about understanding another person's thoughts. Words may be a useful aid in communicating thoughts, but the words themselves are not communication.

Communication is the means by which the thoughts in one person's mind become the thoughts in another person's mind.

Although the following description may seem quite detailed, understanding how communication works is important if it is to be consistently effective. Communication is a multi-step process involving a sender and a receiver. Effective communication depends on each step being successfully accomplished, although rarely does either party consciously recognize that the steps are occurring.

Step One – The Thought: The first step in the communication process is for the sender to formulate a thought to communicate. If the thought is unclear, fuzzy or imprecise in the sender's mind, then it should be no surprise that the attempt to communicate it will result in a different thought in the receiver's mind. A thought needs to be clear in the mind of the sender before it can be effectively communicated to someone else. The sender needs to know what they want to communicate <u>before</u> effective communication can occur. Sometimes communication fails because there has been an attempt to communicate before the message is formulated. This happens especially when emotions are high and words are spoken "thoughtlessly."

Step Two – Encoding: Thoughts cannot be transferred directly into the mind of another person. The intended message must be converted into a medium that can be sent to the other person – the thought must be encoded. Encoding is the conversion of a thought into words, signals, signs, sounds, facial expressions or other forms of body language. The "code" chosen for the message must be common to both parties for communication to be effective. If the sender encodes the message into Russian, but the recipient speaks only Spanish, the message will not be communicated. It is the sender's responsibility to ensure the "coding" used can be understood by the recipient. To communicate with a child, a parent must encode the message in a way that the child can understand.

The more precise the message needs to be, the more precise the encoding will need to be. Encoding normally involves some form of language and words. However, encoding may be a facial expression and a nod that expresses pleasure and approval without any words being spoken. Many messages will require the careful choice of precise words in order to be effectively communicated.

Additionally, how the message will be understood depends on a large number of factors beyond the words, including the setting, vocal tones and body language that accompanies the words. If words and body language are not consistent, then the message will be unclear or confusing. Encoding includes consideration of when and how the message will be communicated.

Modern internet based communication methods often fail to be effective because incomplete thoughts are transmitted with incomplete encoding. It is no surprise that the message intended by the sender is often different from what the receiver understands.

Step Three – Transmitting: The sender transmits the encoded message. This includes written or spoken words along with other non-verbal aspects.

Step Four – Receiving: The receiver hears, reads, observes or perceives the transmitted message.

Step Five – <u>Decoding</u>: Decoding is the process of transforming the coded message into a thought in the mind of the recipient. Having received the message, it must be processed by the hearer to understand the meaning intended by the sender.

Step Six – <u>Feedback</u>: - For communication to be complete, the sender needs confirmation that the message they intended is the actual message received. Feedback consists of a reverse communication process. The receiver now has a thought (as a result of the message received), encodes it and transmits it back. The original sender receives the message, decodes it, forms a thought and compares it against the original thought intended to be transmitted. If the first thought and the last thought are the same, the communication has been successful. If the thoughts are different, then the sender needs to repeat the process until the feedback the original receiver provides matches the original sender's original thought. Feedback is essential to ensure that the message received is the same as the message intended to be sent.

Communication has been successful only if the thought in the receiver's mind is the same thought that the sender intended to convey. Most people mistakenly associate communication with only steps three and four – speaking and hearing. They consider communication effective if words have been spoken by one and heard by the other. Sometimes people think they have communicated if they have said something without caring if the other person actually heard. Effective communication only occurs if all six steps are accomplished.

This explanation is admittedly tedious and complex to describe something that occurs hundreds of times each day without conscious thought. However, understanding the parts of the communication process is helpful in avoiding failures in communication. Care given to each step of the communication process will improve effective communication and will enhance one's marriage significantly.

Understanding the six steps in communication may be of little value and considered unnecessary when communication seems to be working well. However, you will think much differently when your spouse has smoke coming out of their ears and you do not have a clue as to why. Often-times, poor communication is a major contributor to life's problems. Understanding he steps of communication aids in the effective communication which is often needed to resolve problems.

Each step of the communication process presents its own set of challenges. A small miss-step can result in a huge misunderstanding. A few illustrations may be helpful.

Carefully encoding the message is vital. The sender must find common ground with the receiver.

A mother writes the word "NO!" on a piece of paper. Every time her non-verbal toddler approached the hot stove she holds the paper up for him to see. Ridiculous, indeed. The toddler may understand the word "NO!" when it is verbalized. He may even understand the shaking of Mother's head, the wagging of her extended index finger or a gentle slap on his own hand, to mean "NO!" But it is quite unlikely that the toddler would recognize the written word "NO!" Written language is not common ground shared by the toddler and mother. The sender of the message must find common ground by which to communicate.

Care must be used in transmitting or delivering the message. A message will not be communicated unless it is effectively dispensed.

To yell 'Dinner is ready.' across the yard to one mowing the grass and facing away from the one yelling will not communicate the desired message. This is obvious. However, it is common to attempt to communicate without completely having securing the attention of the receiver. The more important the message the more deliberate one needs to be in ensuring that the receiver is staged to "get it" before it is delivered.

The responsibility for effective communication is not something that lies solely on the sender. The receiver needs to exert effort to understand. This includes dedicated attention being given to the sender. For a high rate of success, both the sender and the receiver need to give effort to the process.

One of the peculiar things about marriage is that familiarity becomes fertile ground for misunderstanding. Communication between spouses often occurs through the subtleties of looks, body language or partial verbalization. The more familiar the people, the less likely care will be given to ensure effective communication. The more time spent together the less likely active and focused listening will occur. The result is that, instead of working hard at communication in marriage, the tendency is to become complacent, lazy and assuming. Because the spouse is familiar, assumptions frequently overrule what is actually said. This inclination makes it all the more needful to work hard at communicating in marriage.

Biblical Communication

The Bible has much to say about communication. Some of the more significant aspects of what the Bible says about communication are summarized below.

Christians are to be slow to speak and are to use words which are purposefully chosen.[83] The book of Proverbs is filled with statements that assert that the one who speaks much and without thoughtfulness is a fool. One is to think before speaking. Thought is to be given not only about what is going to be said, but also

83 James 1:19-20, {This} you know, my beloved brethren. But let everyone be quick to hear, slow to speak {and} slow to anger; for the anger of man does not achieve the righteousness of God.

to why and how. Consideration is to be given to the impact the words spoken will have on others.

That which is spoken is only to be the truth.[84] Obviously lying is sin. Lying is always sin and will be very harmful to any relationship in the long run. Likewise, deceit will eventually destroy trust, which is foundational to marriage. This does not mean that the truth is to be boldly and brazenly asserted without regard for the other person. No, the truth is to be spoken with and motivated by love. There are many ways to say the truth. Some of them are shotgun blasts and others are back massages. Speaking the truth does not mean that every thought has to be spoken. Frequently, it is best to say nothing - to overlook a fault and to suffer wrong without a word.

Words that are motivated by love are designed to benefit the other person. Loving words are spoken with the goal of building up the other person, not tearing them down.[85] Such concern and care is only possible when there is humility. When there is a quarrel, the tendency is to make one's point by belittling the other person with sharpened words crafted into dagger like thrusts.[86] There is no place for this in the life of the Christian. There is no place for this in the relationship of husbands and wives who call Christ their Lord.

Words are to be spoken out of gratitude.[87] When people are filled with gratitude, the words they speak show it. As Christians we have much for which to give thanks.

The words of Christians are to demonstrate the fruit of the Spirit of God rather than to be an instrument of the flesh.[88] What one says is evidence of what is in their heart.[89] The ability to control what is spoken comes from being filled with and controlled by the Spirit of God. Control of the tongue is the apex of self-control.[90] To practice self-control over what is said, one needs to fill their heart

---

84 Ephesians 4:15, but speaking the truth in love . . .

85 Ephesians 4:29-31, Let no unwholesome word proceed from your mouth, but only such {a word} as is good for edification according to the need {of the moment,} that it may give grace to those who hear. And do not grieve the Holy Spirit of God, by whom you were sealed for the day of redemption. Let all bitterness and wrath and anger and clamor and slander be put away from you, along with all malice.

86 Proverbs 12:18, There is one who speaks rashly like the thrusts of a sword, But the tongue of the wise brings healing.

87 Ephesians 5:3, But do not let immorality or any impurity or greed even be named among you, as is proper among saints; and {there must be no} filthiness and silly talk, or coarse jesting, which are not fitting, but rather giving of thanks.

88 Read Galatians 5:16-26 and notice how many of the deeds of the flesh are related to speech.

89 Matthew 15:18-19 "But the things that proceed out of the mouth come from the heart, and those defile the man "For out of the heart come evil thoughts, murders, adulteries, fornications, thefts, false witness, slanders." See also James 3.

90 See James 3.

and mind with that which is good.[91] In essence, Christian maturity is being able to think in a right way, resulting in speech that is pure and proper. Such maturity comes as one replaces the world's thoughts with Christ's thoughts, thereby becoming conformed to the image of Christ.[92]

Anger associated with conflicts must be dealt with before bed time.[93] The origin and resolution of most marital conflicts involve communication. Conflicts, often create anger in one or both spouses, make effective communication very difficult. The emotion of anger hinders effective communication at each of the six steps in the communication process. Anger produces bad thoughts that should not be communicated. Anger makes it very difficult to encode, deliver or receive messages. Anger overlays each step of communication with a thick layer of hurt feelings, a desire for vengeance and grief associated with the anger.

Unresolved anger carried into the marriage bed easily evolves into a sexual problem. Thus, the downward spiral is well on the way to major difficulties. When morning comes, the previous day's unresolved anger and problems not only remain, but they also have now hardened and intensified. Thus, God in His wisdom, requires that all Christians deal effectively with anger problems prior to going to bed. More often than not, honest Christian communication, including confession and forgiveness, is the only way to resolve such problems.[94]

Effective communication is also closely related to considering others before oneself.[95] To communicate well requires that consideration be given to the other person; to how they will understand, to how they will respond, and to how they can be encouraged. Good communication requires making the effort to put oneself in the other person's shoes and communicating at their level rather than at your own.

There are obvious and well documented differences in the way men and women think and communicate. Although the reasons for the differences may be disputed, that they exist is universally recognized. These differences may be why husbands are commanded "to live with their wives in an understanding way."[96] There are

---

91 Philippians 4:8 Finally, Brethren, whatever is true, whatever is honorable, whatever is right, whatever is pure, whatever is lovely, whatever is of good repute, if there is any excellence and if anything worthy of praise, let your mind dwell on these things.

92 Romans 12:1-2

93 Ephesians 4:26 .".do not let the sun go down on your anger."

94 Conflict resolution has an entire chapter dedicated to it dealing with how to get past anger to effectively communicate.

95 Philippians 2:3 Do nothing from selfishness or empty conceit, but with humility of mind regard one another as more important than yourselves;

96 See 1 Peter 3:7: literally husbands are to live with their wives "according to knowledge" implying that they should grasp that they are different and know how they are different and treat them accordingly – as fellow heirs of God's grace; equals, yet different.

many books on gender differences and some of them may offer some practical value when it comes to effective communications.[97] But caution is advised, as an over emphasis on gender differences can become an excuse not to fulfill God-given responsibilities. Each one must always allow God's Word to be the guiding factor in their life regardless of their natural or genetic tendencies.

There are few things more vital to a marriage relationship than the ability to communicate effectively. Communication requires much effort. It is highly recommended that husbands and wives set aside dedicated times for communication. This need not be a formal or forced "Let's talk!" time but rather a time dedicated together without distraction or "doing." It can be over morning coffee or after the kids are in bed. Turn off the TV, the radio, and the computer. Set aside the newspaper, the book, the cell phone and the tablet. Be just two people together attentive to each other.

God has communicated with us in His Word, and He expects His children to communicate with Him in prayer. As those who are made in God's image, people have the ability to communicate. In marriage, communication can become a tremendous asset or the source of tremendous trouble. The determining factor will be whether or not both spouses are willing and committed to effectively communicating with each other.

---

97 The author would recommend the idea of communicating by means of word pictures as presented in book *Language of Love* by Smalley and Trent.

Chapter 10
WIVES: How to Be a Godly One[98]

Of all the relationships in life, marriage is perhaps the most proficient at highlighting weakness, sin and character defects. People are often able to put on appearances at work, school and church; but eventually, the true character emerges in marriage. Those who were able to keep up appearances during dating are unable to hide who they are in marriage. The butterfly of dating transforms into the larva of marriage and, as the saying goes, "the honeymoon is over." The close contact and duration of marriage strip away the masks. Sharing the mundane, coping with crises together and enduring the day to day grind of married life reveal one's true character and heart, which the rest of the world may never see.

<u>Potential for Great Joy or Trouble</u>

Marriage brings together two selfish, sinful, self-centered individuals in one household. They share the same pocket book and have overlapping responsibilities but they see things differently. Differences exist in perspectives, experiences and nature.

When a pastor began a sermon by asking, "Why do you who are married have so much trouble getting along with each other?" members of the congregation responded in their hearts in a variety of ways:

- Some said, "Well, we do not have too much trouble!'
- Others thought, "Who told him?"
- A third group pondered, "I wish I knew!"

Marriage is one of those wonderful gifts from God that can seem more like a curse. Sadly, some people get to a point where it seems to be mostly a curse. Over 50% of all marriages ending in divorce reveals that over 50% of married people decided the burdens of marriage outweighed the benefits. Why do some marriages become a "hell on earth"? Why are some people willing to sacrifice everything else to escape a relationship that God created and declared to be very good? Why do over 50% of men end up divorced from the bride of their youth when Proverbs says, "He who finds a wife finds a good thing, and obtains favor from the LORD."[99]

---

98   The reason why the role of the wife is addressed before the husband's role in this book is because the author's oldest three children are girls. This chapter covers some areas common to both husband and wife.

99   Proverbs 18:22

Despite the wonderful potential for marriage to be a blessing, it is equally clear that it can be a thorn in the side. God warns, "It is better to live in a corner of a roof, than in a house shared with a contentious woman," and "It is better to live in a desert land, than with a contentious and vexing woman."[100]

The Bible says that a wife may either be a blessed gift from the Lord or a burdensome annoyance. The question that begs for an answer is "What determines if a wife will be a blessing or a curse?"

After the wedding the pastor told the groom, "Getting married is the end of all your trouble." The young man grinned from ear to ear without a word.

A few months later the young man burst in the pastor's office demanding, "Tell me why you lied to me? You said that marriage was the end of all my trouble. That was a lie! You knew it too, didn't you? I had no idea what trouble was until I got married."

The pastor peered over his glasses with a coy smile. He spoke in a barely audible whisper, "I said getting married would be the end of your troubles. I did not say which end!"

Stories like these provoke chuckles because they reflect common experience. Marriages anticipated with joy, eagerness and excitement produce conflict, hurt, pain, grief, separation, divorce and sometimes even murder. Why?

Although the wife is only half of the marriage, she IS half of the marriage. A wife who understands and seeks to fulfill her God-given role will promote harmony in the home rather than wreaking havoc.

The role of a wife within marriage has become clouded, confused and even lost in all the bantering about equal this and equal that in western society. Opinions about the role of wives are numerous and frequently contradictory. God created marriage. He alone is the authority on the role of the wife in marriage.

At least three factors must be considered when discussing the role of a wife within marriage:

- God designed marriage at creation. (Genesis 1-2)
- Sin and death changed marriage. (Genesis 3)
- Salvation restores marriage relationships. (Ephesians 5)

Marriage is God's Idea

God created mankind as male and female. He established the relationship between

---

100   Proverbs 21:9, 19

them as husband and wife. Marriage was established before sin entered the world. God declared that the whole creation, including marriage, the role of the husband, the role of the wife, and their relationship, was very good. A correct understanding of marriage begins with consideration of the original creation prior to sin. All other instructions about marriage roles are founded upon the original design within creation.

Recall that during the sixth day of creation, something was not good. God said "It is not good for the man to be alone."[101] There was not found a "helper" suitable to or corresponding to man. The man was not complete without his counterpart, the woman. It was only after the woman was created and marriage roles were established that God declared everything to be very good.

The woman was specifically created to be the man's helper. The term "helper" is not belittling. This is a word most often found in Scripture referring to God being a help to His people. God being a "helper" to His people does not imply that He is, in any way, inferior to them. Likewise, using the term "helper" to describe a wife does not mean that the wife is inferior to her husband. But, by God's design, they do have different roles.

God gave the wife a specific role in relationship to her husband. She was not created totally independent of the man. She was created to be a helper corresponding to the man. The first woman was created to be man's counterpart, his associate. She was his wife.

By the design of God's very good creation, the woman as helper was placed in a subordinate role to the man. While many today would label such a statement as "sexist," it should be remembered that God Himself said that all creation, including marriage and the "helper" role of the woman was "very good." If God says this arrangement is "very good" but others disagree, one of the two is wrong – and it is not God.

A wife's "helper" status in marriage is reflected in the balance of what the Scripture teaches about marriage. The New Testament commands the wife to be submissive and in subjection to her husband, would be expected of a helper. The commands to be submissive simply echo God's design and stated purpose in creation. The wife being in submission is God's good design, not the oppressive fabrication of chauvinistic men. This design existed before sin impacted the world or marriage; thus as God declared it to be, it is very good.

Subordination and submission is universal, not something unique to wives. Submission is a quality that is good, right and pleasing to God in every person. Jesus pleased God by having a submissive relationship with God the Father. He was not less than God but submitted Himself to the will of the Father. The same

---

101   Genesis 2:18

type of relationship exists in marriage. The wife is one with her husband but at the same time in submission to him. Throughout creation, whereever God delegates authority, appropriate submission to that authority is commanded and expected. Marriage just one of many human relationships where submission is expected by God.

God's design is for a wife to be her husband's helper, assistant, partner, and associate. It should be her goal to make her husband successful and to help him accomplish his goals.[102] In doing so, she will be helping herself. The wife is no longer one as an individual; but with her husband, the two are one within the marriage. When the wife does good for her husband she is doing good for herself.

<u>Sin Causes Trouble for Marriages</u>

All difficulties in marriage is the result of sin entering the world as described in Genesis 3. Marriages suffer because of the fall of mankind. Exactly how sin changed marriage is frequently misunderstood and misrepresented.

Many wrongly assume that God created the man and woman equal partners in marriage. Likewise, it is also often assumed that a wife's required submission is the result of sin. As a result of these wrong ideas, the solution to marriage problems is thought to lie in establishing and maintaining equality between men and women in marriage. This perspective is contrary to what God says in the Bible. Striving for equal rights is actually one of the consequence of sin. Fighting for equality instead of the wife humbly submitting is actually the source of many marriage problems.

Understanding the outcome of what happened in the Garden of Eden is essential to a proper view of marriage. The result of what happened there explains why marriages are such a struggle today.

After the man and the woman sinned, God spoke to the serpent, to the woman, and to the man regarding the consequences of sin. Of particular interest to the relationship between wives and husbands is what God had to say to the woman. God told her, "I will greatly multiply your pain in childbirth, in pain you shall bring forth children; yet your desire shall be for your husband, and he shall rule over you."[103] A common understanding of this verse goes something like "Because of the fall, women will have great pain in childbirth; but they will still have a physical attraction to their husbands."

While this seems to capture much of the thought of the verse, a more careful look reveals clues as to why there is such conflict within marriages. The last phrase of this verse curiously states that the woman's husband will "rule over" her. One

---

102 At the same time, it should be noted that a loving husband will be sensitive to his wife and they will form their goals together. See the chapter "Husband's: How to be a Godly One."

103 Genesis 3:16

might assume that such an assertion is simply a restatement of the original created order. Instead, the statement is a significant deviation from the original design.

The woman's "desire" may have a physical dimension, but it is also in contrast to the fact that her husband would "rule over" her. The word "desire" means to run after, to run over, to overflow. The result of sin is that the woman would seek to rule over, to overflow, to dominate her husband. This effort, God says, will be frustrated because the husband would rule over her. Sin resulted in the woman no longer being content to be the man's helper. Instead she would seek to be his master. God created the woman to be in submission. Sin resulted in her unwillingness to be in submission.

There is only one other place in the Old Testament where both the words for "desire" and "rule over" are found together. God told Cain a very similar thing:

> "If you do well, will not {your countenance} be lifted up? And if you do not do well, sin is crouching at the door; and its desire is for you, but you must master it." (Genesis 4:7)

The issue with Cain was who would be the master of his life. God told Cain that if he did what was right, he would be his own master. Yet, if Cain continued to do wrong then sin would be the master. Cain did not follow God's counsel to do right, allowed sin to master him, and killed his brother. The main idea of the word "desire" in both the contexts is striving for and establishing control.

The other part of the curse on the woman was that her husband would rule over her. The phrase "rule over" is a deviation from the creation design. Instead of providing loving leadership as God intended, the consequence of sin is that men would dominate and oppress women. He would now rule as a despot in a crushing way rather than lovingly caring for her.[104]

So the tension in marriage is not part of the original creation with the man as the leader and the wife as the helper. Marital problems are the result of two deviations from the creation design as a consequence of sin: 1) the wife will want to rule rather than to help, and 2) the husband will dominate the wife. This conflict is sometimes called "the battle of the sexes," and it underlies the women's equal rights movement and the universal oppression of women by men.

There cannot be two masters and harmony. When two people are striving for control, conflict occurs. God made it very clear in creation that the man was to be the leader and the wife was to be the helper. After sin entered the world, the woman would be constantly striving for the control. The wife's natural inclination to rebel against the authority that God has placed over her is one of the major

---

104 The husband's proper treatment of his wife is covered in the chapter "Husbands, How to be a Godly One."

contributors to marital conflict. Sin damaged God's original creation design for marriage. However, salvation provides a remedy for marital conflicts.

<u>Salvation Brings Restoration of Relationships</u>

Salvation reverses sin and its consequences in many respects. The damage done to the marriage relationship can be remedied on a case by case basis through individual salvation. As each person submits to Christ in salvation, they gain victory over sin. In salvation, relationships can largely be restored to what God intended in the original creation. This happens in individuals one person at a time. Significant measures of restoration can occur in all relationships, including marriage.

The answer to the question "What is the ideal design for marriage?" is found in marriage prior to sin entering the world. The original design, which was declared by God Himself to be "very good," was one man and one woman in the relationship and roles as designed by God who created them.

The New Testament teachings of Jesus and the apostles are based on the creation design for marriage before the fall. Solutions to marriage problems are found in the wisdom of God's Word. Peace and harmony in marriage will be experienced as individuals become realigned with God's will through the grace and forgiveness found in faith in Jesus.

In this matter, Ephesians 5:18-6:6 provides specific instructions to husbands, wives, children, masters and slaves. These instructions are part of an explanation about what it means to be filled with the Spirit.[105] Being filled with the Spirit enables individuals to walk in a manner worthy of their calling in Christ.[106] The result of walking according to Christ's calling and being filled with the Spirit is to bring praise and glory to God.[107] In other words, the life of the saved person is to be empowered by the Spirit of God, consistent with the Word of God, with the result that God is glorified. Salvation is very practical. Salvation transforms most every area of life, including spousal relationships in marriage. Christian wives who are filled with the Spirit will obey the New Testament teaching for wives, resulting in a relationship with their husband that will approach the creation design prior to sin damaging marriage.

The instructions to wives in Ephesians are consistent with the rest of the New Testament instructions given to wives.

---

105 Ephesians 5:18 And do not get drunk with wine, for that is dissipation, but be filled with the Spirit,

106 Ephesians 4:1 I, therefore, the prisoner of the Lord, entreat you to walk in a manner worthy of the calling with which you have been called,

107 Ephesians 1:6,12,14 *salvation is* . . . to the praise of the glory of His grace

Wives, {be subject} to your own husbands, as to the Lord. For the husband is the head of the wife, as Christ also is the head of the church, He Himself {being} the Savior of the body. But as the church is subject to Christ, so also the wives {ought to be} to their husbands in everything. (Ephesians 5:22-24)

The larger context of this passage includes the idea of all believers being subject to one another.[108] For the wife, emphasis is placed on being subject to her husband. The submission of the wife to her husband pictures the church's submission to Christ. Correspondingly, the church's submission to Christ is the pattern which the wife is to follow in serving her husband.

The word submission, which is translated "be subject" in this passage, is often used in a military setting. It literally means "to be ordered under." The idea includes being arranged in ranks under the direction and leadership of a commander. It also includes the concept of being obedient to the will of the commander, whether expressed or implied. Submission is a matter of the heart, not just outward obedience to meet the minimum standards. Heart-submission recognizes authority as God-ordained and acts accordingly, in submission to God.

Submission demonstrates the appropriate level of respect for the husband.[109] The husband's greatest need from his wife is to know that she respects him. This respect is evidenced as she comes alongside in a supportive helper role, seeking to make him successful. Submission will be a struggle in the best of marriages and it will be a greater challenge when husbands are not "worthy" of respect. However, the worthiness of the husband does not change the wife's responsibility to submit.

Unbelieving Husbands

Some women have good husbands and marriages. A few may even have very good husbands and marriages. Many, though, have husbands and marriages that leave much to be desired. What is a wife to do when her husband is either unsaved or disobedient to God?

Some assert that the wife's degree of submission should correspond to the husband's love and obedience to God. Is this what God says? What does God expect the wife of an unbelieving husband to do? What does the Scriptures say is the duty of the wife when the husband is unloving? How should a wife respond to a husband who is rude, inconsiderate and selfish?

In the best of marriages, diligent effort is required by a wife to meet God's expectations. Rebellion against authority is natural. Submission only comes supernaturally. Even when a husband is good, kind and gentle and he sacrificially

---

108 The command to "be subject" is found in Ephesians 5:21 and is implied in 5:22. Actually, "being subject" is one of the results of being filled with the Spirit as commanded in Ephesians 5:18

109 Ephesians 5:33 ."..and let the wife see to it that she respect (fear) her husband."

loves his wife, the wife will still struggle to submit. Sin's curse is that the woman will want to be the boss.

The biblical command for a wife to be submissive is completely independent from what the husband does or does not do. God's expectation for wives does not change whether the husband is saved or not. God expects the wife of an unbelieving and disobedient husband to submit to her husband, the same as He expects the wife of a believing husband. There are several places in the Bible where the requirement for this type of unconditional submission is made very clear.

> In the same way, you wives, be submissive to your own husbands **so that even if any {of them} are disobedient to the word**, they may be won without a word by the behavior of their wives, as they observe your chaste and respectful behavior . . . the hidden person of the heart, with the imperishable quality of a gentle and quiet spirit, which is precious in the sight of God. (I Peter 3:1-4) (**emphasis added**)

The wife with a husband who is disobedient to God and His Word is told to humbly and quietly be in subjection to her husband. The instructions to wives here is part of a larger context that deals with submission of Christians in general. 1 Peter 2:13 says Christians are to be submissive to all authorities. This includes submission to government and submission of slaves to masters. Christ's submission to the Father is discussed as an example to be followed. The instructions to wives in 1 Peter 3:1 begins with the phrase "In the same way." Wives, in the same way as Christ was submissive, be submissive. The description of Christ's actions in the midst of suffering unjustly is held as an example for the wife to follow.

This type of submission displays a gentle and quiet spirit[110] which was demonstrated by Christ who "while being reviled, He did not revile in return; while suffering, He uttered no threats, but kept entrusting Himself to Him who judges righteously;"[111] This type of submission applies to servants regarding their masters. "Servants, be submissive to your masters with all respect, not only to those who are good and gentle, but also to those who are unreasonable."[112] The word "unreasonable" literally means "to be crooked or perverse or twisted."

Submission is not dependent upon the worthiness or the actions of the one to whom you are submitting. Submission is an act of the will based upon the command of God. Submission is required for wives and for all who are under authority. This is because all authority is established by God.[113]

---

110 1 Peter 3:4

111 1 Peter 2:23

112 1 Peter 2:18

113 See Romans 13:1-2

Special Considerations Regarding Submission

Submission to God is always appropriate. Submission to God appointed authorities is the rule; however, there is a narrow and limited exception. There may be times when obeying God requires disobeying earthly authorities. This may include governments, husbands, parents or even church officials.

The Bible clearly states the principle that if submitting to human authority would cause one to sin, then God should be obeyed rather than incur sin.[114] Caution must be urged at this point. It is human nature to rebel against authority. Rebellion is a sinful attitude that looks for justification not to submit. Every effort should be made to obey the authority without sinning. Effort is needed to obey both the human authority and God if at all possible. This may include some creative thinking, making an appeal to the authority, or submitting a request to do something slightly different. Yet, if it comes down to the point where one must either disobey God or the authority, it is right to choose to obey God. This too should be with an attitude of submission to the authority, not rebellion.

While it is beyond the scope of this discussion, it should be noted that women should not be expected to place either themselves or others in physical danger, including their own children. Seeking assistance from the church or even the civil authorities is appropriate at times.

Learning From the Older Women

Being a good and submissive wife can contribute much toward harmony and happiness in a marriage, but the loftier goal in submitting to one's husband is bringing glory to God.

- God is glorified in the wife's obedient submission.
- God is glorified in the testimony her submission provides.
- God is glorified in marriages that demonstrate the love and submission that exists between Christ and the Church.
- God is glorified when the wife sets an example of submission for her children and others.

Conversely, a Christian wife failing in her God-given responsibilities will bring dishonor upon God, His Word and the church. Since this is so important and it does not come naturally, Paul instructed the older women to encourage and train the younger women in these matters.

---

114 For example, this principle is stated is found in Acts 5:29. But Peter and the apostles answered and said, "We must obey God rather than men."

Older women likewise are to be reverent in their behavior, not malicious gossips, nor enslaved to much wine, teaching what is good, that they may encourage the young women to love their husbands, to love their children, {to be} sensible, pure, workers at home, kind, being subject to their own husbands, that the word of God may not be dishonored. (Titus 2:3-5)

Ideally, women would learn how to be good wives and mothers from their own mothers. But sometimes, the mother's example is neither good nor godly. Thus, the responsibility falls upon those within the church to help younger women in their roles as wife and mother. These instructions are directed to older women for the benefit of younger women. Older women are to:

- Encourage Generally - by teaching, training and setting an example. The word "encourage" means to have a sound mind. By sharing insights and experiences, the younger women can be given hope that they can fulfill their responsibilities; and thus, be encouraged to try.
- Encourage Love for Husbands. This is not speaking of the self-sacrificial love which God has for us. The love spoken of here is the friendship and affection that wives need to feel toward their husbands.[115] A wife needs to learn how to be her husband's friend and companion. Love which is affection is often the byproduct of the sacrificial type of love.
- Encourage Love for their Children. This too includes the idea of being friends with their children. Again, the word love refers to that warmth and affection associated with a friendship relationship. This friendship does not erase the woman's authority as a parent.[116] Instead it is focused on being able to understand, relate to and help the child as a friend.
- Encourage as helper and wife under her husband's authority. She is to be morally pure, sensible, diligent in her homemaking, and kind.

The above discussion about being a godly wife can be summarized by saying, "The role of the wife is to be a submissive helper to her husband."

Marriage is a relationship between two people. The wife is only part of the equation for a harmonious marriage relationship. How she contributes to the marriage can make the relationship a tremendous blessing or a tremendous burden. However, the husband has an even greater responsibility to make the marriage pleasing to God. As the leader in the family, in many ways the husband has a greater opportunity to make the marriage successful.

---

115 The word used in Titus for "love" comes from two words: man and friend (philos). The word "philos" means to be dear, a friend, fond. The idea is that the wife is to be the "friend of her man"

116 See the author's book *Children: Raising or Ruining?* for a discussion about the importance of parents understanding their children and being friendly to them without abdicating parental authority.

Chapter 11
HUSBANDS: How to Be a Godly One

Typically husbands blame their wives for the problems experienced in marriage. But many, if not most, instances the husband's marital troubles are largely his own fault. The biblical role of husbands is broadly known yet superficially understood. Perspectives on the leadership of husbands are often distorted.

The story is told of the husband who had spoken sharply to his fat wife. The outraged woman had then chased him all over the house with a broom. Finally, the man sought refuge far under a low bed. She could not follow him because of her plumpness. "Come out from there at once Henry, do you hear!" she panted in fury, poking at him with the broom handle.

"I shall not!" he declared stoutly, "I will be master in my own home!"

* * * * *

There had been another family quarrel. The man mumbled aloud, "A man's a fool to get married. A husband leads a dog's life."

"You said it!" agreed the wife heartily. "He growls all day and snores all night."

* * * * *

One husband boasted, "When I have an argument with my wife I always get the last word, 'Yes dear!'"

Many problems in marriage are the result of misunderstanding the nature of marriage and the husband's responsibilities within the marriage.

One husband defined a wife as "the woman who will stick by your side through all the trouble you would never have gotten into if you had not married her in the first place."

Although both wives and husbands have been cursed by God because of sin, salvation provides the means to overcome the curses. For Christians, marriage can approximate God's original design as each spouse fulfills their responsibilities. More often than not, the husband's failure can be blamed for the pitiful state of his marriage.[117]

Excesses and Extremes

God intends the husband to be the "head of the home." Many problems in marriages can be traced to misunderstanding what it means to be the "head." The tendency is to slide into the ditch on either side of the "authority" road.

In the ditch on one side of the road is the assumption that being the head is a license to be a monstrous monarch who treats his wife like dirt. He claims the crown, demands unquestioning obedience, and rants and raves without any consideration for anyone but himself. Suggestions are ignored. Hints are hated. Questions are suppressed though rationalization or outbursts of anger. He wipes his feet on his wife and gives no thought to her needs. This may be man's mania but it certainly is not God's design. However, this extreme is the direct result of sin's curse that stated that the husband would "rule over"[118] his wife.

On the other side of the road is the ditch of the mustard colored mouse who has a backbone the consistency of warm gelatin. He assumes responsibility for nothing. He allows, if not requires, his wife to take the lead in everything. When he musters up all his strength to take a stand for something he thinks is important, he immediately caves in under the weeping and gnashing of teeth of the scornful woman. This is not what God intends either. This too is the result of sin in the garden. God said the wife would desire, that is to rule over over her husband. Many men find it easier to avoid conflict and let their wives run everything.

The two extremes are purposefully exaggerated to illustrate the point. Yet these descriptions portray the degree of reality in many, if not most, marriages. Either the husband "wears the pants" by brute force and intimidation, or he allows the wife to wear them with little or no resistance.

Lead or Be Led

Much of the conflict and strife within marriages involves a struggle for control. God created the man and the woman placing them in a relationship which He designed. God designed the woman at the husband's side as a "helper." As noted previously, the word that our English translations render "helper" is not in any way a belittling term. Most often the term is used of God and the help that He

---

117 The modern "liberation" of women gains them greater share of the responsibility of marriage failures. As women, along with society in general, fail to give any heed to God's design and purpose for them in marriage, they run over their husbands and refuse to submit to God.

118 See the discussion about the consequences of sin in the previous chapter where it describes the phrase "rule over."

provides to His people in time of distress or trouble. Thus the woman is not lesser than the man, but is designed to fill an assistant position to her husband.

When sin entered the world, the relationship between the man and the woman drastically changed. Sin resulted in both men and women seeking a role that God had never intended when He created them.

After the fall, the woman was destined to be discontent with her created position alongside the man as helper. Instead she would seek to overrun her husband rather than to willingly submit to him.[119] The result is that, although God has designated that the man should provide the leadership, by nature, the wife wants to be the head.

On the husband's part, sin inclines him to abuse his authority. God told the woman that her husband would "rule over" her.[120] The word used here indicates that the husband would now, as a result of sin, oppress and dominate his wife. Such a domination was the result of sin, not part of the design in creation. The conflicts in marriage are greater than other interpersonal relationships of self-centered people. The conflict in marriage goes beyond "normal" selfishness because it is compounded by the unique struggle for dominance in that relationship.

Some husbands do not accept their God-given role of leadership because they want to "keep the peace." Others do not know that it is their role to lead. Still others have no idea how to be the leader. Whenever the husband's leadership is lacking for any reason, the wife is willing to take the lead. The result is a role reversal with the wife leading and the husband submitting. Although this may seem to be an acceptable arrangement that works in some marriages, it is also the source of much dissatisfaction and discontent for both partners. Many marriages hobble along for a lifetime with such arrangements but often they are much less than they could be.

Limitless Love

The responsibility of the husband is captured in that gigantic little word, L - O - V - E. Consider the commands given to husbands found in Ephesians:

> For the husband is the head of the wife, as Christ also is the head of the church, He Himself {being} the Savior of the body....Husbands, love your wives, just as Christ also loved the church and gave Himself up for her; that He might sanctify her, having cleansed her by the washing of water with the word, that He might present to Himself the church in all her glory, having no spot or wrinkle or any such thing; but that she should be holy and blameless.

119This was discussed in detail in the previous chapter regarding the role of wives.

120 Genesis 3:16

So husbands ought also to love their own wives as their own bodies. He who loves his own wife loves himself; for no one ever hated his own flesh, but nourishes and cherishes it, just as Christ also {does} the church, because we are members of His body. For this cause a man shall leave his father and mother, and shall cleave to his wife; and the two shall become one flesh. This mystery is great; but I am speaking with reference to Christ and the church. Nevertheless let each individual among you also love his own wife even as himself; and {let} the wife {see to it} that she respect her husband. (Ephesians 5:23, 25-33)

The same text that asserts the husband is head of the wife explains exactly what that leadership should look like. The Christian husband should look like Jesus. The role and responsibilities of husbands parallel the character and role of Jesus. The husband is the head of the wife <u>like</u> Christ is the head of the church.

Stop - Ponder this thought:
The husband is to the wife what Christ is to the church!

No matter which way one turns that statement, it is extremely weighty. Becoming a husband demands that he be for his wife what Christ is to the church. Although it is hard for a wife to submit to her husband, the husband must submit to Christ. Part of his submission includes loving His wife sacrificially like Jesus loves His church. There should be little doubt that the husband has a responsibility that far exceeds the wife's to love his wife AS Christ loved the church.

The directive to the husband is weighty. Yet the command to love is simply a reiteration and specific application of what is expected of all Christians. All who would call themselves followers of Jesus are to love like Jesus. (After all, isn't that what 'following' means?)

But I say to you, <u>love your enemies</u>, and pray for those who persecute you (Matthew 5:44)

Therefore, however you want people to treat you, so treat them, for this is the Law and the Prophets. (Matthew 7:12)

This is My commandment, that <u>you love one another, just as I have loved you.</u> Greater love has no one than this, that one lay down his life for his friends. (John 15:12-13)

In this is love, not that we loved God, but that He loved us and sent His Son {to be} the propitiation for our sins. Beloved, if God so loved us, we also ought to love one another. (1 John 4:10-11)

The husband's responsibility to love his wife is like the wife's responsibility to be in submission to authority and to other believers. The command to submit is universal. The command to love is universal. All Christians are commanded to love and to submit. In marriage emphasis is placed on each marriage partner's duty regarding their specific role in the relationship. As Christians, both husband and wife are commanded to love one another and to submit to one another. However in the context of marriage, the emphasis is on the wife's submission and on the husband's love because of their specific roles.

As the head who loves his wife, the husband becomes responsible to meet some specific obligations.[121] The first descriptions of how the husband is to love his wife include:

- Sacrificing for her as Christ did, laying down his life for her. The sacrificial love of Christ brought the church into a holy relationship with Him. This is humility. This is the servant attitude which Christ demonstrated and Christians are commanded to have.[122]
- Perfecting her as Christ prepared the church as a bride for Himself – holy, blameless, without spot or wrinkle. Likewise the sacrificial love of the husband has a sanctifying affect upon his wife. Loving his wife sacrificially will contribute greatly to his wife being a beautiful bride.

There is a powerful implication in this passage. Imperfection in the bride is due to lack of love by the bridegroom. In other words, if the wife falls short, then it is evidence that the husband has not sanctified her. He has not loved her as he should. Admittedly, just as the church is self-willed and is not yet perfect, so too a wife will to some extent reject, and fail to respond to, the love of her husband. But until such time the husband loves his wife as Christ has loved the church, there is room for improvement and reason to lay substantial blame at the husband's feet.

A second analogy presented is that the husband is to love his wife "as his own body." There is no command here to love yourself; rather the clear assumption is that each one already knows how to love himself.[123] Prior to Christ laying down his life for the church, the command was to love your neighbor "as yourself." The new command is to love others "as Christ loved us", that is to love others better than we love ourselves. So, this second analogy to love others in the same way we love our own bodies demands an easier sacrifice of love. However, it is not a bad motivation when directed to others. This is the golden rule to do to others as you would have them do to you.

---

121 There are many other passages that discuss the husband's role. Ephesians is perhaps the most detailed.

122 Philippians 2:3-5 Do nothing from selfishness or empty conceit, but with humility of mind let each of you regard one another as more important than himself; do not {merely} look out for your own personal interests, but also for the interests of others. Have this attitude in yourselves which was also in Christ Jesus,

123 The idea that one needs to learn to love oneself is not a biblical concept. What is called low self-esteem is really a manifestation of self love and pride rather than the opposite, as some would have us believe.

This second analogy takes on a greater significance in marriage than in any other relationship. The mystical truth that "two will become one flesh" within marriage means that the husband loving his wife is actually him loving himself. It is our nature to love our own body, to care for them, to indulge them, to nourish them. Thus the husband needs to recognize that such treatment of his wife is as good for him as it is for his wife.[124] Although a husband may not fully grasp the breadth and depth of Christ's love, he is well familiar with what it means to love himself.

The love of a husband for his wife does not produce some soft-bellied, spineless type of "yes-man." Although love is sacrificial and "other serving," it is not without self-determination and responsibility. The love which Christ has for the church is not determined by the church's whims or desires. Christ's love for the church is expressed by doing what He deems best for her. Likewise the husband, although giving due consideration to his wife's desires, has a responsibility to do what is best for her in every way, but especially spiritually.

In love, Christ sacrificed for the church. He also set an example for her. The husband is to be the servant-leader of his wife loving her and setting an example of love for her. As Christ teaches the church how to love and serve, so the husband sets the example for the wife of how to love and serve. In submission Christ, by obeying Him in these things, the husband is also setting an example of submission for his wife to follow.

Another significant passage for husbands is 1 Peter 3:7. As noted in the previous chapter, the context is all about submission.

> You husbands likewise, live with {your wives} in an understanding way, as with a weaker vessel, since she is a woman; and grant her honor as a fellow heir of the grace of life, so that your prayers may not be hindered. (1 Peter 3:7)

The husband is given two responsibilities: 1) to live with his wife in an understanding way and 2) to grant her honor. The second task will be considered first.

Granting honor relates to individual salvation. The wife comes to God on exactly the same terms as the man: as a sinner saved by grace through faith in Christ. With regards to salvation there is no male and no female.[125] Even in marriage the man is not better than the woman and the woman is not better than the man. God has simply given them different roles in marriage. However, the husband must not overlook the fact that before God, and in eternity, his believing wife is his sister in

---

124 Ephesians 5:28-29

125 Galatians 3:28 There is neither Jew nor Greek, there is neither slave nor free man, there is neither male nor female; for you are all one in Christ Jesus.

the Lord, saved by God's grace exactly like he is. Granting honor means viewing his wife as an equal – standing on level ground regarding sin and salvation.

Additionally, the husband is told to live with his wife in an understanding way. The text literally says "according to knowledge." The differences between men and women seem to be in view here. The term "weaker vessel" is used with regard to the woman. One analogy that is sometimes used to explain the term is that the wife is like a delicate piece of glassware - perhaps an exquisite china cup. Part of the husband's responsibility is to treat his wife with careful consideration, understanding that she is highly valuable, but also susceptible to harm by careless handling.[126] The man is not told to "understand" his wife, but to "live with her" in an understanding way. The emphasis is on action. Although it may be impossible for a husband to fully understand his wife, he can understand her enough that he allows her to be different. He can treat her well even if he cannot figure out what makes her tick.

A third observation about this text is important. The term "likewise" at the beginning of the verse refers the context that emphasizes an attitude of submission to authority. The husband must always remember that he may be head over his wife but that Christ is head over him. The husband is answerable to God for how he cares for and loves his wife. As such, God's expectations are clearly defined for the husband. To misuse or to abuse the authority and position given to him by God is a sin for which the man will answer. Failure to obey the commands in this verse results in a man's prayers being hindered.[127] If the man is not obeying God by loving and caring for his wife, his own relationship with God suffers.

A final note regarding the husband's responsibilities. For the believer, it is the never changing love of Christ that provides salvation and security. Likewise, as the husband loves his wife, he provides her security in their relationship. If the wife does not sense her husband's love, she will be insecure! A wife's insecurity will increase her desire to be in control, because there is a felt need to be secure. A wife's sense of insecurity is the source of conflict and misunderstanding within marriage. The burden is on the husband to love his wife, to clearly demonstrate that love to her, consistently and constantly. Part of living with a wife in an understanding way is understanding what makes her secure. A husband's love for his wife will be demonstrated in very practical ways that will be evident to all, but especially to his wife.

---

126 No attempt will be made here to speculate or elaborate on the differences between men and women.

127 1 Peter 3:8

Chapter 12
CHILDREN: Burden or Blessing?[128]

In marriage one thing usually leads to another. Until recently, the one thing marriages usually led to was children. With few exceptions, until the last half century, it was assumed that when people got married they would soon have children, and they would have a number of them. Today however, having children is viewed as a choice that people make.

A brief history leading up to the current views will be helpful. In the wake of the Second World War, the birth rate in the United States escalated, resulting in what is now called the baby-boom. This so-called boom gave rise to concerns about possible over-population. Development and promotion of various means of birth control occurred parallel to two other social trends - the women's liberation movement and the sexual revolution. Soon, sex education programs were implemented within the public education system teaching "safe sex" rather than moral issues associated with sex. Organizations formed and began to promote birth control through education and distribution programs. Having and raising children soon came to be viewed not only as a choice, but also as a great expense and financial drain on families.

Today there is no baby boom in any industrialized nation.[129] Indeed, the birth rate in America is slightly less than two children per family. Birth control has become almost universally accepted and a common practice among Americans regardless of their religious affiliation. Questions about whether birth control is good or bad are seldom asked.[130] Few people, even Christians, stop to ask if God has something to say about children and what our attitude toward having them should be.

Christians need to evaluate everything carefully including this matter of birth control and children. We need not only to examine what we do, but also to seek to understand our heart's motivation. We need to question that which is

---

128   This chapter primarily discusses attitudes associated with having children and decisions associated with having children. The author's book *Children: Raising or Ruining?* is recommended as a resource for a biblical perspective on raising children

129Global fertility rates are in general decline and this trend is most pronounced in industrialized countries, especially Western Europe, where populations are projected to decline dramatically over the next 50 years. Source: USA CIA https://www.cia.gov/library/publications/the-world-factbook/rankorder/2127rank.html

130 The Roman Catholic church is a noted exception

assumed to be okay. We need to ask, "What does God say about this?" and "What does God say about that?" A couple questions that are seldom asked today are "How many children should a couple have?" and "What is God's perspective on birth control?"[131]

One Man Sought Answers

A young father began to ask these questions about having children of almost every sincere Christian man he met. He sincerely sought to know God's will regarding having children. He asked pastors. He asked Christian leaders. He asked his parents. He asked his Christian friends. He ask the elders in the church he attended. He asked the administrators and teachers of a Bible college. The more he asked, the more apparent it became that most people had not even considered the questions. Some thought the questions were funny and made jokes. Others thought the questions were irrelevant. Some considered it to be a subjective and personal question to be answered between each couple and God alone.

Frustrated with trite and thoughtless answers, the young father sought out the writings of Bible expositors and supposed experts on the family. Disappointment came again. He discovered the subject was glossed over without giving serious consideration to the basic question, "What does God say about having children?" Thus the young man turned to the source document itself seeking to search out the answer from God's Word, the Bible.

Unlike that father, this chapter will begin with the Bible. There is not an abundance of direct teaching on the subject, which may in part explain the experience of the young father described above. However, numerous Bible passages that have implications that need to be integrated to give the whole picture. Admittedly, reaching conclusions based on this type of study can be considered neither definitive nor authoritative. Consequently, the observations and conclusions offered are intended to provoke thought and consideration.

God is certainly concerned about having children. Christians wanting to please God will at least wrestle with the issue. They will not just assume that cultural norms are consistent with biblical truth.

---

131   The sexual revolution has led to homosexuality becoming increasingly socially acceptable. By 2013 several states have legalized homosexual marriage and a significant number of churches have accepted or endorsed as good what God clearly says is a perversion and sin. It is likely that in the not too distant future most people will assume that homosexuality is acceptable and questions will no longer be asked, much like the issue of birth control is today.

Be Fruitful and Multiply

> And God blessed them; and God said to them, "Be fruitful and multiply, and fill the earth, and subdue it; and rule over the fish of the sea and over the birds of the sky, and over every living thing that moves on the earth." (Genesis 1:28)

Among God's instructions to the first man and woman were to be "fruitful and multiply, and fill the earth." This command was issued when they were the only two people on the earth and was prior to sin. However, it was part of God's original intent that the union of the man and woman result in children. The terms "fruitful," "multiply" and "fill" seem to imply an abundance of children. This command was issued prior to the fall. However, the same command is twice repeated to Noah after the flood.

> And God blessed Noah and his sons and said to them, "Be fruitful and multiply, and fill the earth. ... "And as for you, be fruitful and multiply; Populate the earth abundantly and multiply in it." (Genesis 9:1,7)

Again, it should be noted that the population of the earth was only 8 people when Noah got off the ark. Yet it is noteworthy that the command is the same before and after the entrance of sin. Further, it might be observed that with the entrance of sin came death, and with death came the greater need to be fruitful and multiply if mankind was to fill and subdue the earth.

Some object to applying these commands to today's societies, citing supposed overpopulation and an inability to grow enough food or otherwise support the earth's population. Such objections neglect to take important facts into account. Overpopulation is not, and never has been the problem. The inability for people's basic needs to be met is the result of erroneous views of God and of unchecked human injustices. The issue is not overpopulation but is rather ungodliness, corruption and human greed.[132]

Children are a Blessing

The story is told of a long line of eleven lively children boarding a bus followed by a haggard looking woman. "Whew!" cried the bus driver, "Are those all your children, or is this a picnic?"

---

132 It is ironic that some developed nations have so restricted childbirth out of concern for the cost of raising children that they are now facing financial crisis from not having enough young laborers to support their economy. Some nations are even providing financial incentives for families to have children.

"They are all mine alright," snapped the woman, *"and believe me, Bud, it's no picnic."*

Whether it is one child or eleven, many believe that children are "no picnic." Having children is discouraged as being expensive,[133] burdensome and restrictive. Some say it is irresponsible to have children because there is not enough food or enough room in the world. The negative information about having children is sometimes subtle and other times blatant. This view of children is often related to the idea that personal happiness depends on material possessions. The message given to us is that you have to make a choice between having kids or having nice things.

God's perspective on children presents a very different picture. From cover to cover, the Bible directly states and frequently implies that children are a gift from God and a blessing to the parents. For example:

> Behold, children are a gift of the LORD; the fruit of the womb is a reward. Like arrows in the hand of a warrior, so are the children of one's youth. How blessed is the man whose quiver is full of them; . (Psalm 127:3-5)

It is difficult to determine exactly how many arrows made a full quiver.[134] The precise number is not the point of the psalm. The point is that children, even an abundance of children, are a gift and blessing from God.

Throughout the Old Testament, this concept is repeated. Abraham was to be blessed by God. A significant part of that blessing was the birth of Isaac who would become a multitude of nations.[135] This promised blessing saw fulfillment, at least in part, when about 70 descendants of Abraham went into Egypt and left there four centuries later numbering over 600,000 adult men.

The covenant that God made with Israel included blessings and curses. Obedience to God and the covenant would result in God's blessing.

> And all these blessings shall come upon you and overtake you, if you will obey the LORD your God. Blessed {shall} you {be} in the city, and blessed {shall} you {be} in the country. **Blessed {shall be} the offspring of your body** and the produce of your ground and the offspring of your beasts, the increase of your herd and the young of your flock. Blessed {shall be} your basket and your kneading bowl. Blessed {shall} you {be} when you come in,

---

133One recent study stated that it now costs about $1.5 million to raise a child from birth through college. Online financial calculators are available to supposedly calculate the cost of raising children. Some suggest that the cost of raising children is greatly overinflated for political reasons.

134 At the time when this psalm was written, quivers are estimated to have held between 3 and 150 arrows.

135 Even Ishmael was to be blessed by God. Part of that blessing was his becoming a great nation of many people. (Genesis 17:20)

and blessed {shall} you {be} when you go out. ... The LORD will command the blessing upon you in your barns and in all that you put your hand to, and He will bless you in the land which the LORD your God gives you... **And the LORD will make you abound in prosperity, in the offspring of your body** and in the offspring of your beast and in the produce of your ground, in the land which the LORD swore to your fathers to give you. The LORD will open for you His good storehouse, the heavens, to give rain to your land in its season and to bless all the work of your hand...if you will listen to the commandments of the LORD your God, which I charge you today, to observe {them} carefully (Deuteronomy 28:2-13) (**emphasis added**)

Note that twice God promised children as a blessing to Israel. When taken in association with the blessing of the ground and the offspring of beasts, it is also apparent that it is numerous children which are the result of God's blessing. The converse also holds true. Disobedience by Israel would result in God's curse coming upon them including a lack of children.[136]

As an interesting exercise read the above verses once again. This time ask yourself two questions as you read.
1) Which of the blessings do people want today? and
2) Which of the blessings do people today NOT want?
It seems that people of all cultures and societies want cattle, fields, return on investments, profit from labor . . . all these blessings but one - not children. Especially not many children. Many people would consider having a large number of children to be a curse. God includes many children in the list of blessings. Why is it this way? It is possible that society's view of children and an abundance of children, is different from God's view? Is it possible that Christians have blindly adopted an ungodly society's view on children rather than seeing children as God does, as a blessing?

Some would suggest that many children were a blessing because of the agricultural nature of the nation Israel. More children meant more farm workers. There may be some legitimacy to this perspective. However, God's view of children being a blessing does not seem tied to this.

The covenant with Israel is different from His relationships with the church and individual Christians. However, the fact that people want all the blessings promised to Israel except for perhaps, children should cause us to examine whether our values line up with God's values.

---

136 See Deuteronomy 28:18ff for example. It does not necessarily follow that infertility is the result of a curse from God or the result of sin in a woman's life. There are numerous examples of women who were unable to have children through no fault of their own.

The Old Covenant and Sexual Uncleanness

The Israelites were given instructions regarding several areas of sexual practice. Premarital and extramarital sex were condemned, as were homosexuality, bestiality, and incest.[137] Additionally, regulations were given to the Israelites regarding the sexual relationship between a man and a woman within the marriage union. Of specific interest is Leviticus 15:19-24, where husbands and wives were commanded to refrain from sex during menstruation, and for seven days after.

While a variety of reasons are offered for such a restriction, one thing becomes clear when considering fertility and children. It is common knowledge that the time a woman is most likely to conceive begins about seven days after her monthly menstruation ends. The Israelite man and woman who obeyed God would abstain from sex during menstruation and for seven days thereafter. The result would be resumption of sex would occur during the most fertile time of the woman's cycle. It seems God commanded this practice to ensure that their obedience would make them fruitful, at least in part.[138]

This observation is made simply to point out that God intended the Israelites to be blessed by many children. He also provided laws for them to follow as one means of ensuring an abundance of children. If they obeyed Him, they would increase their likelihood of having more children.

New Testament Teachings

The New Testament presents even less direct teaching regarding children than the Old Testament does. However, like the Old Testament, it presents children in a very positive light. Below are two simple observations.

Jesus seemed to have a special spot in His heart for children. He even rebuked the disciples when they were hindering the children from coming to Him.

The qualifications for leaders in the church make mention of their children as if to assume that the man who leads the church will have children.[139]

---

137 Leviticus 18:6-18,22-23; 20:10 & Exodus 20:14

138 Christians are not required to obey the covenant God made with Israel. However, it is instructive to understand the results of following these laws and how it relates to the promised blessing of abundant children.

139 For example see 1 Timothy 3:1-7; As a father of seven and being a pastor, it seems that God has used my children to teach me more about God and His relationship to us than any other one thing. Although it is not required that a man must have children to be a church leader, there is much to be learned by having them. The author's book *Children: Raising or Ruining?* devotes an entire chapter to lessons that parents learn from having children.

Possible Biblical Reasons for Limiting Children

Like the rest of this chapter, the following is offered primarily to provoke thought. The questions and suggestions are not intended to impose restrictions but rather to promote consideration of what God considers best for His children and most pleasing to Him.

It is an interesting exercise to ponder how some of our common experiences would be different if sin had not entered the world. For example, what would the woman's fertility cycle be like if sin had not entered the world? It is doubtful that it would be the same.

Without the effects of sin, would a woman be fertile as frequently as is commonly experienced? Healthy women are fertile for four to seven days each month from roughly the ages of 13-55. Potentially a woman of child bearing age could have a child every year, or at least every two to three years.

Scripture seems to indicate that there may have been some significant changes in this area as a result of sin.

> To the woman He said, "I will greatly multiply your pain in childbirth, in pain you shall bring forth children; yet your desire shall be for your husband, and he shall rule over you." (Genesis 3:16)

A literal rendering of a portion of this verse is "I will greatly multiply your pain and your pregnancy (conception)." It appears that as a result of sin, the woman's ability to conceive was greatly multiplied. This multiplication may include that a woman would potentially have more children. Perhaps this curse included more frequent conception than God originally intended. It seems possible that sin increased fertility, resulting in more children being born.[140]

Since salvation is the reversal of the results of sin, it may be reasonably suggested that there is a valid reason to intervene in the conception process. This is similar to accepting medical processes to avert physical death. Death is not natural but rather is the result of sin.

A second possibly legitimate basis for using conception control is the pursuit of unencumbered service of the Lord. Paul gave instructions regarding the benefits of singleness that may potentially be applied to having children as well.

> But I want you to be free from concern. One who is unmarried is concerned about the things of the Lord, how he may please the Lord; (1 Corinthians 7:32)

---

140 Indeed, the woman's monthly menstruation cycle is sometimes called the curse. Consider that prior to sin, the woman likely did not have menstruation cycle since menstruation is, in some way, the death of a potential life.

Understanding that the primary purpose of marriage is companionship and not procreation is important.[141] With children come responsibilities. With the responsibilities come distractions that limit one's ability to serve the Lord. However, there is perhaps no greater opportunity to serve the Lord than by serving your own children. In many cases an increase in ministry may actually come through having children, rather than in the absence of them.

A third possible consideration is the well-being of the mother or child. There are times when a pregnancy may endanger the mother's life. Sometimes factors beyond a person's control may result in a high probability of deformity or genetic diseases. Such situations should be weighed carefully regarding conception control.

Motivation is the Heart of the Issue

For the Christian, the motivation is to bring glory to God.[142] Glorifying God is accomplished by humble and submissive obedience to Him as instructed in His Word. God glorifying humility recognizes that God's revelation takes precedence over human reason. What God says is more important than what any person thinks. Sometimes it is helpful to first identify what we think and then compare that to what God says.

SUGGESTED EXERCISE:
- LIST on a blank piece of paper all the reasons why women have abortions.
    * * * * * Complete your list before continuing! * * * * *
- CIRCLE the reasons for abortions that are also the reasons for using conception control.
- PLACE AN "X" by each reason that rejects the idea that children are a blessing from God.
- PLACE AN "S" by each reason that is potentially sinful and INDICATE the sin (selfishness, pride, greed, materialism, etc.).

Admittedly, in most cases, conception control and abortion are very different. Yet, acceptance of birth control has a relationship to the widespread practice of abortion. The intent is not to suggest that birth control and abortion are equal. The question is about identifying motivation. If underlying motivations are essentially the same, then there should be cause for concern. Birth control needs to be given thoughtful consideration rather simply accepted without any thought.

---

141 The chapter that deals with the sexual relationship within marriage discusses the purpose of sex as well as the issue procreation.

142 1 Corinthians 10:31 Whether, then, you eat or drink or whatever you do, do all to the glory of God.

Types of Birth/Conception Control

Birth control is practiced in a variety of ways. Some couples choose to limit sexual encounters between spouses to periods of non-fertility.[143] There are also physical means of birth control which attempt to prevent physical contact of the sperm and the egg, thus averting conception. Chemical means of birth control may either inhibit conception or cause the woman's body to reject the fertilized egg. Rejection of a fertilized egg is a chemically induced abortion. Surgery is also used to eliminate possibility of conception. This may include minor surgery in the man or a variety of surgery options for the woman.

The term "birth control" is somewhat misleading. Technically, abortion is a form of birth control. Abortion as birth control is killing a child, and that is clearly wrong. Any acceptance of birth control by a Christian would better be considered to be "conception control,, the preventing of pregnancy rather than the terminating of pregnancy.

If tinkering with reproduction is considered acceptable at all, then the means of birth control should be carefully chosen. Only those means that prevent the conception from occurring should be considered. Those that result in an abortion or rejection of the fertilized egg are not acceptable options.

Training the Child

The focus of this book is limited to primarily marriage, and dating as it leads to marriage. However, children are often a significant part of marriage.

The author has another book that deals extensively with parenting and raising children from a biblical perspective.[144] Raising children is discipleship. Parenting is intensive discipleship. Discipleship is the process of instructing, reproving, correcting and training in righteousness.[145] Discipleship includes evangelism and purposeful edification. The goal is that the child will be trained to live a godly life in an ungodly world.

---

143 This method is neither healthy for the marriage relationship, nor is it very effective.

144 The author's book Children: Raising or Ruining? provides a complete discussion of parenting and raising children.

145 2 Timothy 3:16-17 describes the Word of God as being adequate for these purposes.

Chapter 13

MONEY and DEBT:
Gravel in the Gears of Marriage

It is well documented that money tops the list as a source of conflict in marriage. Not surprisingly, finances is also the reason most frequently cited by people for getting divorced. If tension and conflict over money could be eliminated from marriages, then a major victory would be won in the struggle for harmonious and peaceful homes.

People enter marriage with differing views on finances. Each person has a strong opinion about saving, making purchases, borrowing, giving, etc., although their opinion may not be clearly formulated or articulated.

Much of what each marriage partner believes regarding money has been learned from observing family and through cultural influences. Few people enter marriage with a clear understanding of what the Bible teaches about money. Many have never even considered that God cares deeply about all these things. Fewer still have sought to learn what God says and have adopted an attitude toward money that is not consistent with what the Bible teaches.

It is no wonder that money evokes conflicts in marriage. Each person enters marriage holding to their personal subjective view of money and finances. These view are often tenaciously held because they represent their family heritage. A change in their view may be considered a condemnation of what they have learned through example from their parents. Spouses also share a common resource pool, if not a common bank account. Natural selfishness is unwilling to overlook a spouse's devotion to financial priorities different than their own. Everything is in place for a "perfect storm," making financial conflict almost inevitable.

The solution to potential or actual conflict over finances is for both spouses to know what God says and to submit to Him in this area.

Submitting to God will include several interrelated biblical dynamics, including:

- viewing money and material things from a biblical perspective.
- establishing priorities by husband and wife working together.
- distinguishing needs from wants.
- adopting a biblical view of giving.

One significant contributor to marital financial pressure is debt. Borrowing money is a cultural norm. Although the bride and groom may have different perspectives on debt, it is likely that one or both will enter marriage in debt, or at least assuming debt is a normal part of life.

The rest of this chapter presents a challenge to consider assumptions about debt in light of biblical principles. As with other topics addressed in this book, the goal is to provoke thought and careful consideration of the topic. If both spouses embrace God's perspective on money and debt, a major source of marital discord will be eliminated.

A Personal Journey

For many years the author and his family have attempted to follow the principles outlined in this chapter. Their story includes a journey from indebtedness, to financial poverty and then to material abundance. An appendix at the end of this book entitled "God Never Promised Me a House!" chronicles their personal experience. For them, trusting God with personal finances has been very practical, even when obeying God seems contrary to the prevailing wind of financial wisdom.

Basic Biblical Principles

First, a couple of basic questions about God and money:

- What does God promise us regarding money? and
- What does God expect of us regarding money?

Many people, perhaps most, grew up in families in which financial principles were caught rather than taught. The financial values and practices adopted and embraced are those learned from parents and associates by observation, rather than by direct instruction. Few children seem to receive direct and specific instructions regarding finances. Even fewer children receive instruction purposely and clearly based on the Word of God.

Surprising to some, God is very interested in how money is viewed and spent. He is interested in the offering plate, in money sent to missionaries and in giving to some worthy causes. But God's concern about how money is spent is much deeper, broader and basic than those things. It would not be an exaggeration to say that God is interested in how every cent is spent. How money is spent reveals what is important to a person. The use of money reveals heart priorities. There should be no doubt that God is interested in priorities of the heart.

Attitude Check

A teaching intern at a well-known Bible college had aspirations to become a pastor. He claimed to know the secret to staying out of trouble in the church. He said, "If you want to avoid trouble in the church, never talk about the three M's: Marriage, Money or Music." Although avoiding sensitive issues may bring a superficial peace, Christians should take seriously everything that concerns God. God certainly has much to say about money and our attitude toward it.

As with many of the subjects pertinent to marriage, it is important to try to set aside previously held notions about money. Starting with a clean slate enables acceptance of scriptural teaching without prejudice. Those already committed to financial habits may have difficulty changing when confronted with God's Word.

The attitude of one who wants to follow God should be "What does God say is best? What brings God the most glory?" It is common to have a different attitude that asks, "What does God allow? How close can I get to the line without crossing it?" It seems that many are "line pushers" when it comes to finances. Instead of striving to do what is best, they seek to do what can be tolerated. The ability to understand the truth of God increases in proportion to the heart's willingness to obey. So what has God promised regarding money?

<u>God Promises to Meet Our Needs</u>

Basic needs include food and covering according to numerous texts in the New Testament. Because God promises that He will meet these needs, the believer is encouraged in several ways according to Matthew 6:19-34:

- Be concerned about accumulating heavenly treasure rather than earthly treasure. (v 19-21)
    - Where treasure is, the heart follows. (v 21)
- A person can serve either God or money, not both. (v 24)
    - There is no need to worry about food or clothing; God promises to provide these. (v 25-34)
    - Seek God's kingdom and righteousness instead of worrying about what God has already promised. (v 33)
- Needs will be met on a daily basis so do not be concerned about tomorrow. (v 33) (this is <u>daily</u> bread in Matthew 6:11)

God will provide for the daily needs of His children. His children are to trust Him to meet those needs and to concern themselves with God's kingdom. The contrast between the earthly and heavenly treasures are related to the "treasure of the heart" and the master of life. The person storing treasure on earth has a heart affection for things of the earth rather than the things of God. The person worrying about material needs is serving money rather than God. Money becomes the master.

Financial debt has implications regarding affections and who is the master served.

God Disperses His Unlimited Wealth According to His Will

Is it easier for God to give a person a nickel or a million dollars?

The answer to this question is apparent. God has unlimited resources and it is equally easy for Him to give someone a million dollars as it is for Him to give them a nickel. Right? So, if God wants to give someone a nickel, they will have a nickel. Right? If God wants to give someone a million dollars, they will have that too. Right? Of course, God may give you either of these through hard work, or through a gift or by some other legitimate means.

But if a person who only has a nickel wants a million dollars, is it right for him to lie, cheat or steal to get it? No, because God says those things are wrong. More fundamentally, the person who does those things is not trusting God to give them what He wants.

So, if a Christian has their basic needs met and they want something more, what are the implications if they borrow money for something God has not given them?

God Expects His Children to Be Content

The Bible contrasts contentment and love of money. They are at opposite ends of the spectrum of possible attitudes toward money and material things.

> . . . *false teachers* . . . suppose that godliness is a means of gain. But godliness actually is a means of great gain when accompanied by <u>contentment.</u> For we have brought nothing into the world, so we cannot take anything out of it either. If we <u>have food and covering, with these we shall be content</u>. But those who want to get rich fall into temptation and a snare and many foolish and harmful desires which plunge men into ruin and destruction. For the <u>love of money</u> is a root of all sorts of evil, and some by longing for it have wandered away from the faith and pierced themselves with many griefs. But flee from these things, you man of God, and pursue righteousness, godliness, faith, love, perseverance and gentleness. (1 Timothy 6:5-11) <u>(emphasis added)</u>

These verses emphasize trusting God to meet basic needs, pursuing righteousness and resisting desires to accumulate material wealth. In Matthew 6:19-33, Jesus said not to be anxious. Both texts focus on being content with having the basics of life, food and covering.

Contentment is not the complete satisfaction of every desire. Rather, contentment is being satisfied to the extent that unmet desires cause neither emotional distress nor distraction. Contentment comes when a person's experience meets their expectations. When a Christian expects what God promises, they will get what

God promises and their expectations will be met. Thus they will be content. Contentment is reached by adjusting expectations to match what God has promised. This is faith. Contentment comes when God's promises are believed and expected and then experienced. Expecting more or different than what God has promised to provide is the source of discontent.

If a person has what God has promised, what are the implications if money is borrowed to get something He has not promised?

<u>God Expects His Children to Be Patient</u>

Patience and contentment are related. The one who is content with what God has provided will also be patient to wait for God to give them whatever else they may want. Patience accompanies an understanding that God is the giver all good things.

- God knows what is best for each of us.
- God is able to give as much or as little as He desires.
- God will give to each of us what God wants when God wants.
- God will give according to His wisdom and will.

The fruit of the Spirit includes patience. Patience is a character trait of the one who walks according to the desires of the Spirit.[146] The desires of the flesh are contrary to patience. The flesh wants every desire satisfied completely and satisfied now.

Is borrowing money to get something now, rather than waiting for God to provide patience or impatience?

<u>Trust, Don't Test God</u>

The terms believe, faith, trust and obey are used interchangeably in the Bible. Trust is faith that takes action based upon knowing what God has said. Faith is knowing what God has said, agreeing with what God has said and acting on what God has said – because God is trusted. God, who we know through His word, is the object of faith.

A person may have a sincere, genuine faith in something other than God. Although this is a type of faith, it is not biblical faith. It is not faith in God. Sometimes Christians have faith in something other than God or what God has said. In such cases their faith is without foundation in Scripture. When people "step out in faith" without scriptural basis, they are not really trusting "in God." They are trusting in something other than God.[147]

---

146 Galatians 5:16-26

147 Trusting something other than God to do what God does is idolatry.

The person who takes action thinking they are trusting in God, when they are actually trusting in something other than God, is testing God. They expect God to perform according to their unbiblical belief. Testing God is arrogant and quite presumptuous. Like the Israelites who tested God in the wilderness and were punished, those who presume to test God may find that their expectations are not met. Testing God leads to God's displeasure rather than blessings.[148]

A warning against presumption and testing God seems to be the main principle behind the admonition found in James

> Come now, you who say, "Today or tomorrow, we shall go to such and such a city, and spend a year there and engage in business and make a profit." Yet you do not know what your life will be like tomorrow. You are {just} a vapor that appears for a little while and then vanishes away. Instead, {you ought} to say, "If the Lord wills, we shall live and also do this or that." But as it is, you boast in your arrogance; all such boasting is evil. Therefore, to one who knows {the} right thing to do, and does not do it, to him it is sin. (James 4:13-17)

Presumption is assuming on the future. The scenario described in the verses above has several assumptions about the future that are not valid. There is an assumption about the longevity of life. There is an assumption about the success of the business activity.

The admonition is to repent from presumption, to recognize God's control and to submit all of life's activities to His will. "If God allows me to live . . . if it is God's will . . . then . . ." This is not talking about merely adding the words "if the Lord wills" to our plans. This is demanding a change of attitude about life and about presuming upon the future.

Although none of the texts cited above specifically mention borrowing money, each one contains principles that relate to borrowing money. These include:

- God promises to meet basic needs, and contentment is expected when these needs are met.
  - The pursuit and love of money is contrary to contentment.
  - The presence of worry (or the absence of contentment) constitute serving material things rather than God.
  - Borrowing makes one a slave to the debt they owe.[149] Financial obligations force one to make decisions based on debt rather than on the will and leading of God.
- God has not promised material things beyond basic needs.

---

148 See 1 Corinthians 10:1-12

149 Proverbs 22:7 The rich rules over the poor, and the borrower {becomes} the lender's slave.

- ○ Borrowing is done for things beyond what God promised.
- Patience, the fruit of the Spirit, dictates waiting on God to give what God knows is best when it is best.
  - ○ Borrowing is not being willing to wait on God.
- Borrowing is testing God rather than trusting God.
  - ○ Borrowing assumes years of continued life, years of continued health, continuation of ability to work, continued job, etc.

Although none of the above passages say specifically that it is wrong to borrow money, it seems that patience, contentment, faith and trust in God all lean heavily away from borrowing money. God is able to provide in advance if He wants a person to have something. Trusting God to give what He wants, when He wants and how He wants would seem to honor Him much more than presuming on Him and on the future.

Submitting control of the purse strings allows God to control the course of one's life[150], including what is purchased. It seems simple enough - if God has not provided the means to buy something, then we don't need it now and God does not want us to have it now. Once the funds are in-hand we are stewards to use the resources wisely.

Although many so-called practical objections can be raised regarding the position of no debt, it is hard to argue with God. One common objection is the assertion that nowhere in the Bible does God prohibit debt.

Does God Prohibit Debt?

Some, perhaps in defense of cultural norms, would argue that there are no passages that directly prohibit debt. This argument is made despite the principles cited above. Often times, the challenge arises from worldly pragmatism of one who is already deep in debt.

One passage does seem to strongly assert that believers to be free from debt.

> Owe nothing to anyone except to love one another; for he who loves his neighbor has fulfilled {the} law. (Romans 13:8)

The context of this passage is submission to the authorities who have been ordained by God. The verse is specifically speaking about paying taxes and other forms of tribute. However, the verse's meaning does not seem to be narrow. This verse transitions to the fact that believers have a debt or obligation to love one another. The obligation to love one another cannot ever be fulfilled. Believers always have this obligation no matter how much we make payments on it. But

---

150 For example, if God is leading you into full time Christian service, or to relocate, or in some other direction, the existence of debt becomes a hindrance to following God's leading.

beyond the debt to love one another, all the other obligations are to be met and not to be left outstanding.

English translations fail to do complete justice to this verse since it contains multiple negatives making it a very emphatic statement. A very literal translation would go something like this:

"And to no one nothing be obligated, except the one another to love"

The verse says "owe no person." Plus, the verse says "owe nothing." Love is the only thing that is to be owed. Despite interpretive gymnastics that are sometimes done, it is pretty difficult to legitimately come away from a careful consideration of this verse and say it is acceptable to "owe some money to some person in addition to owing them love."

Additionally, it should be realized that financial obligation does not promote love. Quite the contrary, many a friendship has been destroyed because one friend loaned money to another friend. Financial obligation creates tension, stress and pressure. Someone once said, "If you are thinking of asking for a loan from a friend, decide which you want the most: the money or the friend." Although a loan may be appreciated at first, it is common for resentment to arise from the obligation to repay it. And the one loaning the money often experiences resentment toward the borrower because they miss payments, are not timely, or totally "forget" about the loan.

Some hold that Romans 13:8 and the rest of the Scriptures define debt as an obligation currently due which is not met - that is a late payment. It could legitimately be asked, if such an interpretation begins with the "status-quo" or begins with the Scriptures. A late payment is a failure to keep one's word and is, in essence, stealing from someone else. This is obviously wrong and damaging to the testimony for Christ. Debt, on the other hand, is an obligation to pay regardless of when the payment is due. If it is not paid in full then there is an obligation - someone is owed and there is debt.

One last comment regarding Romans 13:8. Although significant, this passage alone does not provide the complete picture on Christian financial practices. The other biblical principles cited stand, regardless of the conclusion reached about Romans 13:8.

Stewardship and Debt

Mature Christians recognize that everything they have belongs to God. They see themselves as stewards of what God has entrusted to them - time, gifts, financial resources, and most significantly, the gospel. Everything is in trust from God to be used for His glory.

Some suggest it is better stewardship to borrow money, thinking it will lead to financial gain and increased wealth in the long run. The specific example often cited is getting a mortgage to buy a house rather than renting. However, even if considered only in dollars and cents, renting may be better stewardship. Home ownership has additional financial obligations beyond the mortgage payment. There is also the compounding of interest. The average home mortgage results in paying 100%-200% more than the sticker price.

Admittedly, in some situations, when only dollars and cents are considered, there may be a financial advantage to buying with credit. Yet there are issues other than just dollars and cents to be considered.

Home ownership, especially when associated with a mortgage, has great potential to foster "treasure on earth" attitudes. Consider the investment in a home for 19 years. People work week in and week out, largely to make the house payment. An emotional attachment naturally comes by constantly having in mind the obligation to pay and by working to pay (this is a treasure-heart issue). What happens when financial trouble results in the inability to pay and the house is lost? The emotional attachment to a house for which cash is paid, even when it requires years to save, may be much less than that constant investment over years.

Additionally, payments on debt tends to enslave the borrower. This too is a heart and treasure issue. Mortgage or no mortgage, material "treasures" can become the focus of the heart's affections. Christians are to seek to store treasure in heaven and not on earth. Any action that causes earthly treasure to captivate one's heart should be guarded against.

Giving and Debt

Christians are to be giving people. They especially are to give to those within the family of God. As stewards, giving is a significant area of responsibility. Since all things belong to God, all things are to be used in ways that glorify Him and to accomplish His purposes.

Habits and patterns of giving to the Lord's work should be established early in life. Giving should be regular and based on what God has provided. Giving is to be generous and directed to those involved in God's work. Giving should be thoughtful and meaningful, rather than just writing a check for 10%. Giving is to come from the heart.

Giving is better than loaning. If something cannot be given away, a person probably cannot afford to loan it. When something is loaned, potential for damage or loss exists. When such damage or loss occurs, relationships may be jeopardized. So, whether something is given or loaned, one's attitude should be that everything belongs to God. Giving contains a blessing; loaning contains a preoccupation with being repaid or with having the item returned. Give without thought for being repaid, and the Lord will repay you.

Taken alone, any of the passages considered here are just one important part of the financial picture of a life that pleases God. When considered together, the picture becomes clear: how a person handles their money is very important to God and it reveals what is important to them.

Living in the Real World

One may ask if it is practical or even possible to live in a way that is totally free from financial obligation. In a theoretical sense the answer is "yes." In a practical sense though, the answer is... well... "almost yes." For example, when the services of phone and electric companies are used, they are used in advance without pre-paying for those services. The service is provided by means of credit, and an unpaid financial obligation is incurred.[151] Technically, that is debt. However, the necessity to use services prior to paying should not lead to the conclusion that all debt is the same, and therefore, going in debt is acceptable.

Financial Discussion Prior to Marriage

Different perspectives about money lead to disagreements that can be a significant contributor to marital disharmony. So, it is important for both partners in a marriage to come to a mutual understanding and agreement about money. Ideally, they will be in agreement because they are both in submission to God.

Below are some questions for discussion that may help those anticipating marriage to avoid future marital conflicts regarding money.

1. Who will handle the money?
2. Who will do the bookkeeping and how?
3. What is your opinion about saving money (how much, how often, for what purpose, how long)?
4. What are your thoughts about credit buying?
5. Will there be a budget? How will that function?
6. Who will buy what? When? How?
7. What can be purchased independently without discussing it with the other spouse? Is there a dollar limit? What about purchasing things outside the budget?
8. Will bank accounts be joint or separate? Why?
9. Will legal ownership be joint or separate? Why?

---

151 The author personally struggled with this at one point in his life and concluded that if the cash resources were available on hand to pay the expected bill then he would "live with it." Another option would be to put money on deposit with the utility to ensure you have always paid for what you use. The use of credit cards may be viewed in a similar way.

10. Will there be discretionary money each week or month for which no accounting will be required or expected?
11. What amount of expenditure constitutes a major purchase?
12. What amount of expenditure should require the mutual consent of both marriage partners?
13. What is your attitude about receiving financial help (gifts and loans) from in-laws and relatives?
14. Are one or both going to contribute to the financial income of the family?

Budgeting in Submission

Budgets are one means of managing finances. Establishing a budget will prove beneficial in a number of ways.

- A budget provides a means of communication between spouses regarding anticipated incomes, expenses and priorities. Having a written budget allows the husband and wife to have a common point of reference regarding finances.
- A budget provides a basis for examining priorities. Often, money is spent on low-priority items while higher priorities are neglected.
- A budget provides a means of tracking expenditures and adjusting priorities. By keeping track of everything that is spent and comparing it against the budget, couples gain a clear understanding of where their money is spent. Not knowing where the money has been spent is often a major source of conflict.
- A budget is a tool to plan how to live within your means and to be able to save for major purchases. Budgeting is a tool that can help you reach material and financial goals without debt.

There are many different kinds of budgets. Some rigid budgets designate specific amounts to different categories based on money available. If the budgeted amount is spent, then no more money is available in that category until the next budget period. This is a good type of budget when money is tight and self-discipline is a struggle. On the other end of the spectrum, a budget can be primarily a tracking mechanism to provide awareness of how much has been spent in each area. If priorities are well established, an abundance of money is available, and each partner is disciplined, this type of budget works well.

No matter what type of budget is used, the goal is to be faithful to use the money God has provided in ways that reflects God's values. Having and using a budget is an important tool to keep finances under control and to minimize marital conflict.

Be Thoughtful and Submissive

The purpose of this chapter is to provoke thought about money. One specific goal has been to provoke thinking about debt in ways that perhaps have not been considered before. It is desired that each reader go to God's Word and study these things carefully rather than taking what has been written at face value. Seek God. Seek to know His perfect will for you. The heart of the matter is to be willing to do what God wants you to do, no matter what that may be. That was what Jesus told the rich young ruler.[152] Give your life to God, and you will have a life that is full and fruitful. May God bless you as you seek to live for Him.

---

152 Matthew 19:16-30

Chapter 14
SHARING RESPONSIBILITIES:
Who is Doing What?

Chuck slouched on the couch while Susan, his lovely bride of two weeks, cleaned up after dinner. As the evening news droned on the TV, Chuck's attention was riveted toward the corner of the kitchen barely visible from where he sat. After a wonderful honeymoon, they had been in their apartment for a week. Now, Chuck wondered if he had made a terrible mistake in marrying Susan. Glaring at the heap of trash in the corner he fretted, "My mother certainly would have taken that trash out long before now. What kind of wife is Susan? What is wrong with her?"

Susan glanced over her shoulder as she placed yet a third paper bag next to the jam-packed trash can. The other two bags were full of trash. She caught a whiff of the chicken bones left over from their very first dinner in their new home a week ago. The smell revolted her stomach. Every day she was tempted to take out the trash, but she did not want to over-step her bounds. She did not want to hurt Chuck's feelings by doing his job. She did not want to make him think that he was not a good husband. Susan thought of her own father and how much she respected him. Each morning her dad took out the trash as he left for work. Susan was perplexed and concerned. "What is wrong with Chuck?"

It is not hard to imagine ending to this story. Some would be peaceable. Some funny. Others quite possibly would be neither humorous, nor peaceable. Many simple misunderstandings often lead to harsh words, hurt feelings, or even tears. If these rifts are not addressed and repaired, bitterness easily sprouts. Marriages may even end in divorce if both parties do not eventually learn to communicate clearly and deal with misunderstandings honestly.

It is a wise saying that "An ounce of prevention is worth a pound of cure." This chapter is intended to offer that ounce of prevention regarding household and family responsibilities. The problem is that each spouse enters marriage with unrecognized assumptions. However, as married life unfolds, small differing assumptions create the potential for significant unnecessary life conflicts.

As in the above story, problems occur when one assumes that the other will do something, and they do not. Predicaments also arise when both assume responsibility for the same task. Many "turf wars" and "neglected fields" can be largely avoided by candidly discussing duties, tasks and responsibilities in advance of marriage. Additionally, agree with your spouse to ask questions rather than rely on assumptions when something does not seem to be working as desired or expected.

Below is a work sheet for couples anticipating marriage. Make two copies of the pages. Independently complete them. Then compare answers. Discuss, negotiate and agree who will do what. This exercise does not create a "law" for how it will be in marriage. It is just a means to stimulate and focus discussion. The purpose is to identify and resolve potential tension points in advance. This exercise may also be helpful as a periodic adjustment to sharing the responsibilities of married life.

One wife humorously insists that her husband has all tasks that begin with the letter "C." She has an amazing ability to manipulate the name of each household task so that it begins with "C." Setting the alarm becomes "clock setting." Giving kids their midnight drinks becomes "children watering." Weeding the garden is titled "cultivating." Mowing grass is "clipping the lawn." Discipline is "correction." Whether this method or another is chosen, there needs to be clear communication between spouses to eliminate needless and trivial conflicts.

Exercise: Who is Doing What?

Instructions: Each one should complete the following exercise independent from their future spouse. For each duty indicate "yes" under the parent in your childhood household who fulfilled the duty. Then indicate your expectation regarding who will fulfill the duty within your own marriage. If you do not know how the parents of your future spouse fulfills the duty, you may skip over that portion. In no case however, should you skip over the portion dealing with your own expectations.

After both have completed the list independently, compare responses. Where difference of opinion occur in the third column, discuss, negotiate and come to some preliminary agreement.

DUTY	Bride's Parents		Groom's Parents		Our Home	
	Wife	Husband	Wife	Husband	Wife	Husband
wash clothes						
wash dishes						
cook meals						
clear dishes						
fold clothes						
clean house						
vacuum						
clean toilets						
change bulbs						
change diapers						
bathe children						
mow grass						
weed grass						
banking						
shopping, food						
pay bills						
gardening						
discipline kids						
trash						
dusting						
mopping						
weeding						
sprinkling						
write letters						
send cards						
devotions						
repairs						
change oil						
minor repairs						
hedges						
milk cows						
gather eggs						
change bedding						
bring in wood						
track budget						
cash checks						
distribute $						
call plumber						
baby bottle						
relative care						
canning						
home schooling						
etc						

Chapter 15
CONFLICT RESOLUTION:
Seeking Peace not Victory

> If possible, so far as it depends on you, be at peace with all men. Romans 12:18

In marriage the question is never "if" there will be conflict but rather, "When?" and "Over what?" and "How significant?" If two living and breathing people have occasion to interact on more than a casual level, eventually there will be conflict. Conflict is inevitable. Every married couple has had conflict: and if they live long enough, they will have conflict again. Some couples have more conflicts than others. Some have conflicts of greater magnitude and duration. Conflict in marriage is normal and sometimes substantial. However, being aware that conflicts will exist and preparing to resolve them will help reduce both their number and magnitude.

On an individual level, conflict is a clashing of interests or ideas usually resulting in an emotional disturbance. Conflicts occur for a variety of reasons.

Sources of Conflict

Sinful People: Broadly speaking, conflicts occur because people are sinful. All people are by nature selfish and look out for their own good. A desire for personal security results in a desire for each one to be in control of their life. Each person is plagued with pride, thinking he knows better than others.

Different People: Conflicts also occur because people are different. Each person is a unique individual, different from any other person. There are different cultural backgrounds, experiences, priorities, perspectives, and thought processes. Any of these differences frequently is opportunity for conflict.

Inadequate Communication: Conflicts frequently occur because people do not effectively communicate. Sometimes it is assumed that the other person understands completely and that they are just being difficult. Sometimes, though, they don't really understand. The assumption is made that "everybody knows that." However, the person who seems to simply be stubborn or "difficult" may not "know that."

Self-Focus: Husbands and wives tend to project their thoughts onto the other without actually expressing them in a way that the other can understand. A wife may assume that her husband understands her feelings. Consequently, she does not effectively communicate her feelings to him. On the other hand, husbands often do not listen carefully to their wives until "the pot has steamed to the point of boiling over." Compounding the problem are busy lives in which people simply do not spend much time together. Even when time is spent together, it is often focused on an activity rather than in an effort to communicate. The resulting lack of effective communication leads to conflict and sometimes distrust.

The magnitude, duration and significance of conflicts can be minimized by anticipating them and by planning what to do when they come. Of course seldom can any specific conflict be planned or anticipated. However, generic planning regarding how to handle conflicts when they arise proves quite helpful.

Failure to work through conflicts has led many couples to walk through the courthouse doors together and leave separately. The number of divorces is a sad commentary upon people's inability to work through conflict. Even sadder, the statistics among professed Christians[153] is little, if any, better than among those who are unbelievers.

Unresolved conflicts between Christians, especially when married to one another, is shameful, considering the resources that Christians have to work through conflict. God has equipped believers with a spiritual arsenal, which is effective in disarming damaging conflict. Ignorance, hardness of heart and pride cause the Christian to contribute to conflict and to live with conflict, rather than resolving conflicts.

The source of conflict can be generally attributed to the deeds of the flesh.[154] That which leads to resolution of the conflict is associated with the fruit of the Spirit.[155] Those controlled by the Spirit of God will be able to work through conflicts. The man who is controlled by the sinful flesh will cause conflict and will be unable to resolve conflict.

Submission Resolves Conflict

A proper relationship to authority plays an important part in conflict prevention and resolution. Like it or not, God has established an order of authority within human relationships upon the earth. Conflict often occurs because there is either a failure to recognize authority or to exercise authority properly. Conflicts occur when bounds of responsibility are overstepped. Sometimes conflict can be

153 Just because someone professes Christ does not mean they are a true Christian. A true Christian walks by faith and in obedience to Jesus. If it were possible to accurately determine the divorce rate among true Christians, it would surely be much less.

154Galatians 5:19-21 Now the deeds of the flesh are evident, which are: immorality, impurity, sensuality, idolatry, sorcery, enmities, strife, jealousy, outbursts of anger, disputes, dissensions, factions, envying, drunkenness, carousing, and things like these, of which I forewarn you just as I have forewarned you that those who practice such things shall not inherit the kingdom of God.

155 Galatians 5:22-23 But the fruit of the Spirit is love, joy, peace, patience, kindness, goodness, faithfulness, gentleness, self-control; against such things there is no law.

resolved simply by allowing the responsible person enough rope either to tie up the problem or to tie a noose around his own neck.

A poster once hung on the inside of a bathroom door depicting a wrinkled old grandma with a rolling pin raised above her head. The caption read, 'Cause I'm the mom, that's why!' While such assertion of authority may not always be the best course to take, sometimes conflicts can be resolved satisfactorily at that level. The resolution lies not so much in the assertion of authority but in the other party submitting to the authority that exists.

When a conflict occurs with one in authority, sometimes the resolution of that conflict is to resign one's self to the fact that they are the God-ordained authority and to submit willingly. By choosing not to make an issue, potential conflict is avoided or existing conflict may be resolved. This is sometimes the easiest and even the best approach to take, especially when the disagreement is over something minor. When honestly evaluated, most conflicts are over matters having minor importance.

For Christians, submission is a two-way street. While the husband is clearly designated as the head of the wife, the husband is also to submit to his wife as a fellow believer.[156] Such mutual submission does not change the authority and responsibility of the husband within marriage, but it does tend to neutralize any tendency toward totalitarian dictatorships that some husbands seek.

Submitting to authority may be nothing more than not asserting your opinion, position, or stance so there is no clash. It is quite possible, and very acceptable, to be of a differing opinion, and yet keep that opinion to yourself. This is neither dishonest nor hypocritical; rather, it is a noble attempt to keep peace and harmony.

Sometimes the gravity of the difference of opinion requires the issue be brought out into the open, discussed and resolved. This may be the case when either the import of the matter or the duration of its impact will not allow overlooking. If something is going to be a long term and constant source of irritation to one party, then it cannot be allowed to fester until one day it explodes.

Although the husband has the ultimate responsibility for decisions in the marriage, the wife is not without recourse. The wife has a responsibility to communicate her concerns and perspective on the issue. The wife should know how to make her case in a clear and firm, yet gentle and quiet manner. Approaching the subject with the right attitude, at an appropriate time, and in a respectful manner makes all the difference in the world. Once the appeal has been made, the wife should be willing to allow slack in the rope, let the decision rest with the husband, and be supportive, for better or worse. Few things get under a husband's skin more than

---

156 Ephesians 5:18, 21 And do not get drunk with wine, for that is dissipation, but be filled with the Spirit, . . . and be subject to one another in the fear of Christ.

repeated mention or harping on an issue. So prepare thoughtfully, communicate clearly, and then rest in the Lord.

A wise and loving husband will carefully consider the counsel of his wife, recognizing his responsibility before God to provide loving servant leadership. When a wife trusts her husband to make the final decision, he is the one who will suffer the agony of defeat or the glory of victory. Such a load of responsibility should make him very careful about making decisions which are contrary to his wife's expressed counsel.

Humility Resolves Conflicts

Humility is the character trait that precedes the act of submission. Humility keeps many conflicts from occurring and resolves many others. A humble person will have conflicts, but a proud person will have many more conflicts. All Christians have a responsibility to humbly put up with others without causing a ruckus:

> I, therefore, the prisoner of the Lord, entreat you to walk in a manner worthy of the calling with which you have been called, with all humility and gentleness, with patience, showing forbearance to one another in love, being diligent to preserve the unity of the Spirit in the bond of peace. (Ephesians 4:1-3)

The unity of the Spirit of God should be more evident in a Christian marriage than in any other relationship on earth. It is each person's responsibility to maintain that unity with humility and gentleness. To do so requires patience and bearing with each other. The motivation is love. As one understands the unconditional and undeserved love of God, then that love can be extended to others.

Humility is having an accurate assessment of one's self, recognizing that God is the source of all good things. Pride is an over assessment of one's self.

> . . . not to think more highly of himself than he ought to think; but to think so as to have sound judgment, as God has allotted to each a measure of faith. (Romans 12:3)

Humility is considering other people more important than yourself.

> Do nothing from selfishness or empty conceit, but with humility of mind let each of you regard one another as more important than himself; do not {merely} look out for your own personal interests, but also for the interests of others. Have this attitude in yourselves which was also in Christ Jesus. (Philippians 2:3-5)

Can a person have conflict with those who are considered more important? Can conflict exist when two people each consider the other person's opinion more important than their own? Can conflict exist when one person is willing to put the interest of the other first? The answers to such questions are obvious. Being obvious does not mean that selfless humility is either automatic or easy. Yet, having the attitude of humility which Christ demonstrated will go a very long way toward avoiding and resolving conflicts.

Humility is the personal characteristic reflected in what is sometimes referred to as the Golden Rule.

> Therefore, however you want people to treat you, so treat them, for this is the Law and the Prophets. (Matthew 7:12)

Conflict usually includes the desire for the other person to come around to your way of thinking. If a conversion of thinking cannot be attained, then at least a backing down from asserting their position is sought. Contrary to such sinful tendencies, the Golden Rule requires that we back down from our position, or at least stop asserting it, since that is what we want the other person to do for us. As Christians, we should do that for the sake of others. If we want others to do that for us, we have an obligation to do it for them.

Extending Forgiveness Resolves Conflict

> And be kind to one another, tender-hearted, forgiving each other, just as God in Christ also has forgiven you. (Ephesians 4:32)

It would be nice to think that there will never be conflicts in marriage. It would also be nice to think that when conflicts arise, they will be settled in a logical and peaceable fashion without any harsh words or hurt feelings. Neither of these is typical. Conflicts often lead to volcanic-like vents of anger and words flying like shrapnel from an exploding hand grenade.

Once someone has "lost it," there is often no way to reverse what has been done. An outbursts of anger and harsh words cannot be retracted nor can their damage be undone. Forgiveness remains as the only positive and profitable option. Granting and seeking forgiveness is required.[157] Forgiveness is not erasing it from the memory. Forgiveness by erasing it from the account. Forgiveness is a commitment not to bring the issue up again or to hold it over the other person for any cause, at any time. Forgiveness is paying the price of the debt that the other person owes you. Forgiveness is the antiseptic and antibiotic that keep the wounds of conflict from being infected. Forgiveness allows each disagreement or conflict to be faced and remedied without the unwieldy baggage of previous offenses.

---

157 See Matthew 5:23-24; 6:9-15; 18:15-35

Apologizing and seeking forgiveness are not necessarily the same. God expects forgiveness to be sought and granted. God never requires apologies. Apologies may fall short of forgiveness. Therefore never say, "I am sorry." Instead say, "Will you please forgive me for _____ (name the specific offense or sin)?" Saying "I am sorry" is not specific. Saying, "I am sorry" may even be a denial of the wrong committed. For forgiveness to be fully transacted, the request requires definitive response such as, "Yes, I forgive you for _____ (name the specific offense or sin)." Having sorrow for the offense should lead to seeking forgiveness.

Strife and division within marriage is always a spiritual issue. Unresolved problems will give the enemy a foothold in the door that will wreak spiritual and emotional havoc. That is why God requires His children to keep short accounts.

> Be angry, and {yet} do not sin; do not let the sun go down on your anger, and do not give the devil an opportunity. (Ephesians 4:26)

Do not hit the sack until the issues are put to rest. That does not necessarily mean that total agreement has been attained. But it does mean that anger and hostility is put away. It does mean that forgiveness is requested, extended and received as needed. It may mean that the issue is still an issue, but it is no longer a conflict with clashing and friction. To be obedient to this command may cost a few hours of sleep. An unwillingness to go to bed until the matter is put to rest first can be a great motivator to work to a peaceable solution.

Resolving Conflict May Require Help

> Does any one of you, when he has a case against his neighbor, dare to go to law before the unrighteous, and not before the saints? Or do you not know that the saints will judge the world? And if the world is judged by you, are you not competent {to constitute} the smallest law courts? Do you not know that we shall judge angels? How much more, matters of this life? If then you have law courts dealing with matters of this life, do you appoint them as judges who are of no account in the church? I say {this} to your shame. {Is it} so, {that} there is not among you one wise man who will be able to decide between his brethren, but brother goes to law with brother, and that before unbelievers? Actually, then, it is already a defeat for you, that you have lawsuits with one another. Why not rather be wronged? Why not rather be defrauded? On the contrary, you yourselves wrong and defraud, and that {your} brethren. (1 Corinthians 6:1-8)

If a Christian couple is unable to work through their differences then it is their obligation before God to seek help from those within the church. God leaves no room for taking a "brother" in the Lord to divorce court to resolve conflict.

Conclusion

Although conflicts are inevitable, they need not be traumatic. Seeking to walk humbly before the Lord in submission to God's authority is essential. Being willing to let minor things slide and working hard at communicating clearly will go a long way toward avoiding potential conflicts. Seeking forgiveness and granting forgiveness will keep each conflict in proper perspective. God intends marriage to be good for all not a "free for all." Being obedient to God to resolve conflicts His way contributes to a happy and harmonious marriage.

Chapter 16
SEX: The Big Picture Perspective

A little girl was puzzled as to her origin. "How did I get here, mummy?" she inquired.

"God sent you, dear," answered the mother using the well-worn evasion.

"And did God send you too, mummy?" was the next question. "

Yes, dear," said mother.

"And did God send grandma and great grandma too?"

Again the answer was yes.

The child shook her head with skepticism. "Do you mean to tell me that there have been no sexual relations in this family for 200 years?"

A time comes in every life when a candid discussion about sex is timely and appropriate. The details and extent of sexual discussions should be purposefully limited in order to be appropriate according to the need.

Unfortunately, in today's culture even very young children are exposed to sexuality by communication mediums and through their peers. Parents should, of course, regulate needless exposure to sexually explicit material to the extent possible. However, it is necessary that children understand modesty and appropriate behavior earlier than in previous generations. Even very young children need to be taught that sex is for marriage only. They also need to learn to be wary of what may potentially be sexual advances. The extent of these discussion depends on the level of exposure that occurs.

A more complete discussion of sex is appropriate immediately prior to marriage. (Although many people are sexually active prior to marriage these days, the assumption in this chapter is that there has been obedience to God. Sex is reserved until marriage.)

A detailed discussion about sex will not be presented in this book. Rather, the intent is to give a few pointers and direction on the subject which will prove helpful to marriages. The updated book, *The Act of Marriage:The Beauty of Sexual Love*[158] by Tim and Beverly LaHaye is highly recommended. Because of the frankness of the sexual content the introduction of that book states, "it should be read only by married couples, those immediately contemplating marriage, or those who counsel married couples."

It discusses intimate sexual function of both men and women. The LaHayes' book will prove very helpful to those anticipating marriage in the very near future and to those who have been married many years.

Sex is Part of Companionship

God created the man and woman as companions for each other. Inherent in God's design for companionship was intimate sexual relations between them. Along with the rest of the pristine creation prior to the fall, God created sexual relationships and said them to be "very good."[159]

Sexual activity should not be viewed as merely a function intended for procreation. Rather, a biblical view of sex seems to emphasize the aspect of oneness and companionship more than procreation. Granted, procreation is also part of God's design.[160]

Sex **IS** Part of the Marriage Package

The sexual act should not be viewed independent from the other aspects of marriage. Sexual relations will affect every other part of a couple's life. A healthy and appropriate sexual relationship is essential to everything else in marriage functioning well.

On the other hand, every part of life will affect the couple's sexual relationship. Stress at work, trouble with children, or difficulty involving finances will carry over into the marriage bed. It is a mistake to think that sex is independent from the rest of life. A satisfying sexual relationship is dependent on what else is happening in a person's world. Marital tension at the dinner table spells trouble in bed and tension and trouble in bed leads to stress and strain out of bed.

Being Sensitive and Serving

Understanding that there are differences in the sexual appetite of men and women is very important. It might generally be said that men tend to desire sex for the sake of sex while women desire sex for the sake of affection. Said another way, sex is primarily physical for men but it has a much larger emotional component for women.

Typically a man can be completely satisfied sexually, independent of precursor events, whether emotionally pleasing or distressing. For many men, sex is sex in an independent moment of time. When the opportunity presents itself, it does not matter if he just extinguished a life threatening fire in the basement or spent

---

159   Genesis 1:31

160 See Chapter 12 – Children: Burden or Blessing?

romantic hours with his wife. Men are ready to have sex at the drop of a hat and enjoy it.

Women seldom enjoy sex to its full potential if it is an interlude to a hectic or stressful day. A wife's sexual satisfaction usually depends on an agreeable emotional context. Romance prior to sex is best for most women. The absence of stress, conflict or emotional pain are important. A wife needs to be emotionally secure in her relationship with her husband for her to enjoy sex.

If the husband and wife quarrel at dinner, when bed time comes, the husband can often have satisfactory sex independent from the quarrel. Yet, if the dinner argument was not properly resolved, the woman will likely be inhibited and even downright cold in her sexual responsiveness.

These differences require constant consideration and understanding on both spouses part. The wife needs to be willing and ready to meet her husband's sexual desires independent of her own sexual desire. The husband needs to be sensitive to his wife and her emotional needs and to seek to bring satisfaction not only in the physical realm but the emotional realm as well.[161]

Ideally, the husband loves his wife as Christ loves the church. In so doing, the continuous sacrificial demonstration of love and affection he shows his wife will provide the security that the wife needs. Such security will prompt affection for her husband which will enable her to also enjoy their sexual experience.

Your Body is Not Your Own

A Christian's body belongs first to God and then to their spouse - truths that have significant implications for sex.

Although sex has mental, spiritual and emotional components, it is largely a physical act of the human body. When a person becomes a Christian, they surrender ownership of their bodies to Christ.

> Or do you not know that your body is a temple of the Holy Spirit who is in you, whom you have from God, and that you are not your own? For you have been bought with a price: therefore glorify God in your body.
> (1 Corinthians 6:19-20) (Emphasis added)

The context of these verses clearly prohibit sexual immorality. Reference is also made to the creation of man and to the marriage relationship in which the two become one flesh. The admonition against immorality alludes to this "one flesh" relationship. The one who has sex with a prostitute becomes "one flesh" with her. Since the Christian is one (spiritually) with Christ, then through immorality Christ

---

161 Philippians 2:3 which says "Do nothing from selfishness or empty conceit, but with humility of mind regard one another as more important than yourselves" is very applicable to sex within marriage."

is joined to a prostitute.[162] Therefore, since you are not your own and because your body belongs to God, you are not to engage in sexual immorality.

God holds title of ownership to a Christian's body by virtue of the purchase price which He paid. Additionally, Christians are commanded to present their bodies back to God for the sake of righteousness and as a living sacrifice.[163]

In marriage, each spouse also relinquishes ownership of their own body.

> Let the husband fulfill his duty to his wife, and likewise also the wife to her husband. <u>The wife does not have authority over her own body, but the husband {does}; and likewise also the husband does not have authority over his own body, but the wife {does.}</u> Stop depriving one another, except by agreement for a time that you may devote yourselves to prayer, and come together again lest Satan tempt you because of your lack of self-control.
> (1 Corinthians 7:3-5) <u>(Emphasis added)</u>

This passage is clear. Each spouse is to meet the sexual needs and desires of the other. Within marriage, each spouse has the right to seek sexual gratification from the other because they hold the title deed to the other one's body. Conversely, each one is responsible to meet the desires of the other, for the sake of the other. Of course, such ownership and demands must be tempered by the other commands and principles in the Bible. To love one another, serve one another and consider one another more important than yourself means that "demanding" sex is never appropriate. However loving, serving and consideration makes "offering" sex always appropriate.

Unilateral withholding of sexual relations is not allowed. The significance of sexual desires is not to be underestimated. 1 Corinthians 7:9 says ." . . it is better to marry than to burn *with sexual desires*." The clear implication is that marriage provide for sexual gratification to eliminate sexual temptation. When married, each spouse bears the responsibility to keep the sexual burning satisfied. Because marriage is the only context for sex that is right, no one but one's spouse can legitimately meet sexual needs and desires. Failure to meet the spouse's desire creates dangerous temptations.

It is impossible to overemphasize that sensitivity to the other person is essential. The loving husband will be considerate of his wife. The loving wife will not needlessly restrict her husband. When one is married, they have relinquished the right to their own body, giving those rights to their spouse. Yet, the possession of

---

162 There are many questions raised here that are beyond the scope of the subject at hand.

163 Romans 6:12 Therefore do not let sin reign in your mortal body . . . do not go on presenting the members of your body to sin as instruments of unrighteousness; but present yourselves to God as those alive from the dead, and your members as instruments of righteousness to God. Romans 12:1 Therefore I urge you, brethren, by the mercies of God, to present your bodies a living and holy sacrifice, acceptable to God,

a "right" does not remove the responsibility to think more highly of the other than of oneself.

Both men and women are prone to sexual misconduct, albeit in very different ways. Women have a tendency to use sex as a mechanism to gain control in the relationship. They withhold sex when they are not getting what they want from their husband or the relationship. They provide sex as a bribe to control their husbands.

Men are often inconsiderate of their wives and push for sex when the wife is not willing. Men, because of the abuses of sex in culture, sometimes develop appetites for sex that are excessive and inappropriate. This is often the result of engaging in pornography and associated sinful behaviors. Both men and women who have been sexually active outside of marriage may have views and desires that are not pleasing to God.[164] In these instances, special effort is required to ensure that the attitudes and sexual practices within the marriage are pleasing to God.

Sex within marriage is normal and good. A healthy sex life is dependent upon and related to every other part of the marriage relationship. Sensitivity to your partner's desires will make sex a satisfying and enjoyable part of the life long relationship with your spouse.

---

164 LaHayes' book deals with some of these matters explicitly.

Chapter 17
COMPANIONSHIP: Being Best Friends

There should be no doubt in anyone's mind that a husband and wife should be friends. They should not only be friends, but they should be best friend.

Apart from blind arranged marriages, most married people probably progressed from being friends, to good friends, to dating, to engagement, and then finally to being married. Friendship is typically the seed that grows into marriage. (A pre-marital sexual relationship alters negatively the dynamics and significance of the friendship aspect both before and after marriage.[165])

Although many marriages begin with some level of friendship, the best marriages nurture that friendship to maturity. The happiest marriages are those in which husband and wife are best friends. This is good for the quality and endurance of the marriage. If your spouse is your best friend, you will not divorce.

Being best friends in marriage does not happen automatically. If it did, marriage would be much easier than it is. Friendship must be cultivated and fostered. In other relationships, friends come and go. Wrongs and hurts may result in someone who was previously a "good friend" becoming just "a friend" or even just an acquaintance. This type of drifting in marriage makes for a miserable relationship and is a contributing factor to many broken marriage vows.

Fostering Friendship

What is a *best* friend? Friends share common interests, enjoy the same activities, and share intimate aspects of personal life. Being best friends may include some of those things but it is best characterized by the desire to be with that person above all others, independent of the activity or surroundings. Friendship is about people, not possessions or activities. All of the other things mentioned are only icing on the cake. Friendship is the cake.

True friendship is built around the person, not likes, preferences or activities. Someone may hate to go shopping or fishing, but if it means spending time with a special friend, the activity becomes secondary and the time becomes enjoyable because of the company. The assumption is that the activity involves interaction

---

165 Sex before marriage distorts the normal pattern of friendship building that usually occurs in pre-marital relationships. Pre-marital sex may actually become a hindrance, rather than an aid, to knowing one another as friends. Sex, apart from the mutual commitment of marriage, tends to exaggerate the importance of the physical relationship over the friendship and companionship. This frequently is detrimental to the intellectual, emotional and spiritual aspects of the relationship.

with the friend. At the same time, it is possible to be physically together but relationally separate. A wife may not like fishing, but as a friend may go fishing with her husband. However, if the husband wades up the stream and leaves the wife sitting alone . . . she may see him but they are not relationally together.

In many marriages there is little friendship because there is little time actually spent relating to one another. Two people can sit and watch TV for hours together and not have interacted for more than a couple of minutes. This creates a false sense of "time spent together." In reality they may have essentially been spending time alone (or time with the TV) while being in the same room. This type of "time alone, together" is well illustrated by the television, but can occur with almost any and every activity.

To spend time together there must be some level of attention given to and focus on the other person. Part of the reason why most wives love to go out to dinner is because the setting allows opportunity for both the husband and the wife to focus on one another. There is no food to prepare, no dishes to wash, no kids to correct, and (hopefully) no phone to answer or TV to watch. It is potentially a time together that they actually spend together.

This description approximates the definition of a "date" given in a previous chapter: "time together plus focus on one another." The together time and mutual focus in dating led to friendship and emotional attachment. The drifting apart in marriages is often because there is neglect of these very simple but important aspects of the relationship. Married people should continue to "date" one another in this way as a means to maintain and strengthen their friendship.

Being best friends with a spouse is a reflection of one's relationship with the Lord. There are willing sacrifices that are readily made because the price is worth it. When friendship exists, the value and pleasure of the relationship outweighs the enjoyment experienced from any particular activity.

Terms like "hunting widow," "fishing widow," "football widow" and more recently, "computer widow" have been coined for the woman whose spouse lacks sensitivity to them.[166] These terms describe husbands who value an activity more than the relationship with their wife. This attitude was depicted on a T-shirt stating, "My wife said that if I go on one more hunting trip that she is going to divorce me." It continued by saying, "I am sure going to miss her!" Although supposedly a joke, it represents the attitude of some. This attitude minimizes the importance of his spouse being his best friend.

Cultivating friendship need not be tedious or expensive. It requires more thought than money. It requires more consideration than cash. It is buying a single flower "just because." It is picking up a favorite candy bar on the way home. It is the card,

166 Women have their own activities which exclude husbands but terms do not seem to have been coined to identify them.

poem or letter. It is the special occasion precisely when there is no expectation for one. It is making that favorite meal and listening to one's heart's desire. It is having special times together.

Being a friend is doing for the other what you would want them to do for you. It is being considerate and kind. It is being open and honest, and yet careful not to inflict unnecessary pain and hurt. It is being thoughtful.

In good marriages, the husband and wife are friends. In the best marriages, the husband and wife are best friends. It is worth the time and effort to cultivate friendship within marriage, because there is no relationship in life where the bonds of friendship can run deeper.

Chapter 18
How to Find a Husband or Wife

Many people want to get married yet find it quite challenging to identify a potential spouse. One evidence of this is the multiplication of internet-based dating services and their widespread use. Why is finding a spouse so challenging and what can be done to make it easier? This chapter offers some answers and suggestions.

Why is Finding a Spouse so Challenging?

There are reasons why finding a spouse is challenging. The young person who is looking for a spouse is venturing out into unfamiliar territory. They have no experience finding a spouse. They are usually trying to make the journey alone. And they have not been taught how to find a spouse. These factors are interrelated and combine to make finding a spouse challenging and even frustrating.

Additionally, choosing a spouse is perhaps the most important earthly decision one will ever make. Generally, the more important the decision or task, the more care is needed; and therefore the greater the pressure to get it right.

There is also often an awkwardness and embarrassment inherently involved in the process. The young person who desires to find a spouse faces an unspoken social stigma hindering them from being open and transparent about their goal. Society does not allow one to reveal, even to those close to them, that they desire to be married.

Although it is generally considered acceptable to be privately looking for a spouse, it is a taboo to openly discuss a desire to be married. Expression of a desire to find a spouse is often equated with being loose or desperate, both having negative connotations. Additionally, those who do make it known that they are "looking for a spouse" often find people with good intentions trying to match them up with unsavory and unqualified people.

Another significant contributor to the challenges facing those looking for a spouse is their own felt need to assert their independence. Cultural norms in western societies allow, and even seem to dictate, that a young person make decisions about who they will date and marry independently. Additionally, many young people who are of the marrying age are ferociously independent, especially regarding this area of their life. Any help that may be available to them is neglected, dismissed, rejected and even disdained for these reasons.

Also, the common idea that there is one, and only one perfect soul-mate causes people to be looking only for their perfect match. This romantic idea results in excluding godly potential spouses from consideration because they do not produce the falling in love feelings society portrays as normal.

The challenges to finding a spouse are a combination of cultural and personal matters that leave the task to an individual with no experience and reluctant to accept help from those with experience.

Christians Face Added Challenges

Christian young people face even more challenges than their non-believing counterparts. In some ways, the more committed a person is to following and serving the Lord Jesus, the greater the challenges become. The reasons for the challenge being harder are good. But knowing they are good and important does not make them any easier.

One of the uniquely Christian challenges is that a relatively limited number of potential marriage candidates exist. A Christian can only marry a Christian, eliminating well over half of the potential candidates. A Christian, depending on their view of divorce, may be unwilling to marry a previously divorced person, eliminating more potential candidates. A Christian who is committed to serving the Lord will further limit their potential selection to only individuals who clearly demonstrate their faith and maturity in their relationship with Jesus.

Christians will have specific and high standards that their potential spouse must meet. The higher the standard, the fewer potential candidates there will be. This makes the challenge for the Christian looking for a spouse greater than the unbeliever. However, these same qualities will greatly increase the likelihood that the marriage will be good.

The challenges facing a young person looking for a spouse are significant. However, there are ways to alleviate some of the difficulties.

Live by High Personal Standards

The standard that a young, committed Christian young person has for a potential spouse is the same standard that they should live by themselves. The potential spouse who meets the high standards of a committed Christian is also going to be looking for someone who meets that high standard. To be considered as a potential marriage partner, there must be obvious faithfulness, commitment and demonstrated service to the Lord.

The person who wants a devoted Christian as a spouse needs to be devoted themselves. The standard by which the potential spouse is measured is the standard to live by.[167] The more faithful you are in your relationship with the Lord, the more likely you are to find someone with the level of commitment you desire in a spouse. Women who develop the qualities of a godly wife, and men who develop godly leadership characteristics increase their desirability as potential spouses.[168]

Be Willing to Communicate and Involve Others

Marriage was created by God as something good. Marriage is very good. Marriage is the norm. If so, then why are individuals so reluctant to make it known that they desire something that God created and is very good? It is obvious that cultural norms are not always best; and often times they are not even good. Christians should be willing to set aside cultural norms in order to do what is good and what is best. Looking for a spouse is one area where following cultural norms makes finding a spouse more challenging than it needs to be.

One of the challenges in finding a spouse is the limited circle of acquaintances and friends each person has. Within that circle of friends and acquaintances there may be few, if any, who could be considered potential spouses for you. However, within the circles of your friends and acquaintances, there may be qualified candidates. By honestly communicating your desire to be married, the likelihood of finding a spouse increases.

Reluctance to communicate one's desire to marry stems from the fact that it opens the door to potential matchmaking. Although matchmaking is viewed with disdain and disgust by many, it is not necessarily bad. Actually, it holds the prospect of identifying potential marriage candidates who otherwise would go unnoticed. Communicating your desire to marry can be limited to potential matchmakers who understand high Christian standards and who know people who may actually be a good match for you. Honest and clear communication on your part will help them know who may or may not be worthy of your consideration. Many people may be well meaning but have no idea what actually makes for a good spouse. These people would be wisely excluded.

Involve Wise Matchmakers

Matchmaking is a third party making a connection between two people with a view toward them getting married. Matchmaking may occur at many different levels, some of which may be more acceptable than others. Matchmaking may be as simple as introducing two people. Or it may be arranging a marriage between

---

167   This is what Jesus meant in Matthew 7:1-2 "Do not judge so that you will not be judged. For in the way you judge, you will be judged; and by your standard of measure, it will be measured to you." Contrary to conventional thinking, judging is not prohibited. Dual standards are.

168   These qualities are in Chapters 10 and 11.

two people who have never met. Or it may fall somewhere between these two extremes.

As Christians, determining who you will marry by dating, or by courting, or by arrangement should be viewed the same. None is more biblical than another. Whether the marriage is arranged by the parents or by those who will be married, the biblical criteria for the spouse is the same. Although forced matchmaking or matchmaking based on wrong criteria is intolerable, it does not mean that all forms of matchmaking should be automatically excluded from consideration.

In many instances, an openness to some level of matchmaking combined with dating or courtship may provide the greatest opportunity to find a suitable spouse. Of course, the acceptability of any matchmaking endeavor depends largely on the spiritual maturity of the matchmaker. Unbelievers and worldly Christians may identify a large number of potential spouses for you, but most, if not all, will be disqualified. The effectiveness of a matchmaker depends on their understanding of what a good match is for the committed Christian and specifically, for you.

Among each person's circle of contacts, there naturally exist individuals who may be especially helpful in finding a spouse. Godly parents, pastors, elders, missionaries and others involved in Christian service usually understand what constitutes a good "match." These people are likely to be spiritually minded. They may have contacts with other spiritually minded people and they have some personal knowledge about you. Communicating discretely,[169] even asking for help in identifying a potential spouse may be a very reasonable thing to do. One of the benefits in involving other people is that some of the initial sorting and screening is already done for you. A recommendation from a spiritually mature individual likely means that the candidate meets some minimal criteria.[170]

However, it should be clearly understood that although someone may initially appear spiritual and godly to a third party matchmaker, they may actually be immature or not even saved. The recommendations stated in the chapters on dating are still very applicable, even when others recommend a person for consideration. It is important that a potential spouse be scrutinized well beyond public appearances and images. Much care is needed to make sure that before you agree to marry someone, you know what that person is really like. After all, you, not the matchmaker, are going to have to live with them all your days.

Location, Location, Location

Christian young people often find themselves in situations where it seems that there are few, if any, potential marriage candidates. Children of missionaries, home

---

169 Discretion is choosing carefully those who will be wise matchmakers. An unwise matchmaker will not help find a suitable spouse and may cause problems for you.

170 Although cultural norms generally dictate that the boy initiates contact for dating, it is completely appropriate for a girl to take the first steps.

schooled children, and children from small towns or churches may think that "there are no good guys or girls" out there. This perspective is perhaps true within their limited circle of friends or acquaintances. This is largely a function of their location and limited associations.

A church with 25 members ranging from 1 year old to 90 years old is not likely to have a wide selection of marrying-age young people. But there is another young person in the same situation, thinking the same thing in a similar small church somewhere – and the two may be a great match. They just don't know that the other person exists. One way for them to meet would be through a common acquaintance who introduces them to each other – a matchmaker. Another way for them to meet would be through a change in location.

There are places where available Christians of marrying age tend to congregate. The person who desires to find a suitable spouse may consider relocating to a place where there is a concentration of Christian young people. Wherever there is a large number of Christian young people it is more likely that there will be others who are looking for a spouse and who may be a potential spouse. These places include Christian colleges, youth groups at larger churches, seminars and conferences, Christian camps, short term mission trips, etc.

Admittedly, enrolling in school or accepting a position of Christian service for the sake of finding a spouse may seem inappropriate. However, if there is a desire to be married there is nothing wrong with that motive; and doing what is needed to meet people is not bad either. Additionally, although there may be dual motives, the committed Christian will be learning and growing and serving in these venues. After all, all things are to be done to the glory of God, including finding a mate.

It is Okay to Expand the Box

It is certainly possible that a Christian young person who desires to be married lives in an isolated cabin, and God could still send them a spouse. However, it may also be that the God-given desire to be married to be fulfilled some action on your part may be required. The person who wants to be a missionary goes to school, applies to the mission organization, and takes steps to meet their acceptance criteria. This is true with many things in life, including education, job training, or even meal preparation. Actions to pursue one's goals are considered completely acceptable in these areas.

However, when it comes to accomplishing the goal of being married, a mystical fog rolls in. Many consider it weird, creepy, or otherwise unacceptable to say that you are looking for a spouse or to take intentional steps to find a spouse. This dual standard which is formed by the world's thinking needs to be evaluated and overcome.[171] Honesty and the seriousness of marriage allow that it is good to want

171 Romans 12:2 seems to apply here. "And do not be conformed to this world, but be transformed by the renewing of your mind, so that you may prove what the will of God is, that which is good and acceptable

to be married, it is okay to admit you want to be married, and it is wise to get mature godly help in finding a suitable spouse.

<u>Trust God! Be Willing to Wait!</u>

Ultimately, God is in control of all things, including finding a spouse. The person committed to the Lord may wait quietly and prayerfully for God to send them a mate. But it is also acceptable for them to let it be known that they are "looking," to solicit assistance from others, and to purposefully put themselves in situations where they can meet others. Some things are unacceptable, though.

It is unacceptable to lower God's standards to find a spouse. God's standard is that a Christian marry a Christian. This cannot be compromised. Individual preferential standards can be careful evaluated, weighed and adjusted. Some people hesitate to commit because they are only willing to marry the perfect mate. Waiting for the prefect soul-mate may lead to overlooking a godly, good and acceptable mate. There are no perfect people and there are no perfect mates. However there are godly people who can be good mates.

Discontent and impatience are not acceptable. Although having a desire to be married can be good, it is not good to be discontent with being single. It is not good to be impatient with being single. Contentment means being satisfied to the extent that one is not distracted or distraught. A person can be content and still have a strong desire to marry. But their life should focus on serving and glorifying the Lord, not on worshiping marriage and doing whatever is needed to become married.

As with all things in life, the Christian should commit themselves to the Lord, wait upon the Lord, and faithfully serve Him as they wait. The desire to be married should include the heart attitude "If the Lord wills." It is much better to remain single than to be in a hurry or to be discontent and to enter into a marriage that may become hell on earth.

---

and perfect."

Chapter 19
The Wedding

Complete this exercise to begin thinking about weddings. You will find it thought provoking and perhaps enlightening.

1. On a blank paper list all the things included in weddings.
2. Underline those things legally required for marriage.
3. Next, circle the things that are biblically required.
4. Finally, draw a box around those things with an identifiable biblical basis and annotate chapter and verse from the Bible.

Weddings - Who Needs Them?

The transition between being single and being married includes a wedding of some kind. As defined earlier, "marriage is a lifelong, divinely established, relationship of commitment between a man and a woman resulting in the two becoming one." The wedding, also sometimes called the marriage ceremony, serves a legal function, a societal function, and a spiritual function.

Legalities regarding marriage ceremonies vary with location. Most places require that the wedding include a voluntary declaration of commitment expressed to a recognized official overseeing the wedding. Those being married must declare that they agree to take each other as husband or wife.[172] When the official and the witnesses sign the marriage license, they are certifying that the two parties made this declaration. Most states consider the marriage to exist upon completion of the ceremony. Some states do not consider the marriage to exist until there has been a sexual relationship (consummation of the marriage) after the ceremony.

Weddings are typically a combination of meeting legal, social, and religious requirements and expectations. The expectations for a wedding vary wildly from culture to culture. Even within the same society expectations vary between families. Careful evaluation will reveal that much, if not most, of what occurs at weddings is based on traditions and social proprieties. These are constantly changing. Consequently, wedding ceremonies can cause strife, struggles, hurt feelings and division because all the different expectations cannot possibly be met.

In American culture today, many people are opting out of marriage altogether. Even people who call themselves Christians are living together finding it somehow

---

172   Beyond agreeing with what the Bible says about lifelong marriage, the content and extent of the vows are culturally and traditionally determined. Ironically, the vows that are made usually far exceed the actual commitment that is being made. Otherwise many marriages would last much longer than they do.

justifiable to live in fornication without being married. This tolerance of sin legitimately calls into serious question whether a person is a Christian or not. However, even people who embrace marriage as right and pleasing to God, commonly ask questions about the need for a wedding ceremony. Because of changing views about marriage, questions commonly include:

- Is a wedding required in order to become married?
- Is a legal marriage required to be married in the eyes of God?
- Aren't weddings just a man-made tradition?

A perusal of the Bible reveals that there are few instructions regarding weddings. The word 'wedding' seldom occurs. It is found once in Psalms, once in Song of Solomon, and about a dozen times in the New Testament. Most of the New Testament uses are in the parables of Jesus. The parables communicate spiritual truths from the well-known wedding practices of the day. The do not proscribe how to do weddings themselves. The only New Testament mention of an actual wedding is in John 2, the wedding where Jesus turned water into wine. In Revelation, there is mention of the "marriage" of the Lamb; the occasion when the Church of Christ will be presented and celebrated as the Bride of Christ.

Other Bible passages allude to what may be called the marriage ceremony,or wedding but they are few.[173] The biblical references to weddings provide a limited understanding that people had weddings, there were various traditions, and it was somehow clear when people had passed from being single to being married. Sexual activity outside of marriage in the Bible is always considered sinful.

<u>Weddings Are Important</u>

There are several reasons why weddings are important for the Christian. Regardless of the form the wedding may take, it serves to make it distinctly clear that two people who were previously single are now married. Being married is not just something that includes the two people involved, but it also includes society and God. For this reason people make vows before a recognized official and the ceremony often includes references to God. In its basic function, the wedding marks the point in time when:

- <u>Those being married</u> make a commitment to one another as husband and wife,
- <u>God</u> joins the two into one, and
- <u>Society</u> recognizes the union. This would include both legal and cultural aspects of what it means to be married.

---

173   Two examples are Isaac and Rebekah and Samson. "Then Isaac brought her into his mother Sarah's tent, and he took Rebekah, and she became his wife." (Genesis 24:67) Samson's botched wedding. (Judges 14)

It is important to understand when people are not married according to the Bible.

- People are not married just because they have sex[174] – there is neither commitment nor social recognition.[175]
- People who live together are not married – to some extent both commitment and social recognition is lacking (otherwise they would get married).[176]
- Homosexuals cannot ever be married – even if they can make a commitment and society grants a legal status, God does not join them together. A wedding does not change this.

Those who believe contrary to the above simply do not believe God. Marriage includes all of these components:

- An expressed exclusive commitment between two people,
- A societal recognition of that exclusive relationship, and
- God's divine joining of the two into one.

The wedding accomplishes two of the essential components required to be married.

<u>Wedding Essentials</u>

As with many things in life, it is important that a wedding accomplish its purpose regardless of the different forms it may take. The function of the wedding is to make a clear transition of a single man and a single women to become married as man and wife. After the wedding, the couple, society and God consider them to be married. This is the function of the wedding. Each aspect of this function is important to the committed Christian.

Christians are commanded by God to be in willful submission to the governing authorities.[177] Unless the government requires something that would be a sin against God, it is necessary that Christians fully comply with the legal requirements of marriage. If the government requires a recognized official, vows, a license, blood test, etc., care must be taken to ensure complete compliance.

---

174 As mentioned previously, it is indeterminate exactly when God joins the two into one. Sex alone does not constitute marriage. However, the sexual union is important and its significance should not be underestimated as 1 Corinthians 6:15-16 makes clear "Do you not know that your bodies are members of Christ? Shall I then take away the members of Christ and make them members of a prostitute? May it never be! Or do you not know that the one who joins himself to a prostitute is one body with her? For He says, "THE TWO SHALL BECOME ONE FLESH."

175 When a child is born outside of marriage, the parents are legally recognizes as having obligation to provide financial and material support for the child.

176 In some states co-habitation has some legal standing as common law marriage.

177 For example Romans 13:1-8; 1 Peter 2:18-3:8

A weddings should include a commitment between the bride and groom. Those with a biblical view of marriage will make a commitment that matches what God says about marriage. Unbelievers will agree to become husband and wife, but the exact view of what that means and the vows that are expressed vary widely. Non-Christian vows will be dictated by tradition, cultural views and religious beliefs. These may or may not contain Christian components.

Witnesses of the wedding contribute to the social recognition of the resulting marriage, as well as meeting the legal requirements. The wedding is incomplete if it does not result in the general public recognizing that the couple is married. Although not highly regarded in modern culture, the exclusiveness of the marriage relationship necessitates that people know that a person is married. The married person is not "available" for another marriage (or another relationship). It was probably for this reason that, until recent times, newspapers published announcements of engagements, weddings and divorces. These announcements were not just gossip. They were part of informing the public of a person's marital status because of its significant relational implications.

Distinctly Christian Wedding

All weddings include a commitment, a legal aspect and a social component but not all weddings are distinctly Christian. So what makes the wedding distinctly Christian? Below are some aspects of a wedding ceremony that distinguishes it as being genuinely "Christian":

- Christian Bride and Christian Groom: A distinctively Christian marriage is one in which both parties are disciples of Jesus, that is Christians. If one or both are not Christian, it is not a Christian wedding.
- Biblical View of Marriage: A distinctively Christian marriage is based upon what the Bible teaches about marriage. The conduct of the wedding communicates the nature of marriage from God's perspective. This aspect necessitates that the official overseeing the exchange of vows a biblical view of marriage and is able to communicate it. Although, a civil ceremony before a civil official can effectively get people married, the deep spiritual meaning of marriage will be lacking.
- Christian Vows: A wedding that is Christian will include vows that are based on a biblical view of marriage. These vows will make lifelong commitments that includes moral purity, love, submission and an exclusive relationship.
- Christ: A Christian wedding will center on Christ. The bride and groom are servants of Christ. Their roles in the marriage are patterned after the love of Christ and their submission to Christ. Marriage depicts the church of Christ. The ability of those marrying to please God depends on each person submitting to Christ and obeying Christ.

- Christian Witnesses: The witnesses of a wedding bear an obligation to hold accountable those making the vows. These witnesses are the tip of the sword, so to speak, for society. Society expects that married people act like married people. The witnesses provide accountability for them to be faithful to their vows - to do what they said they would do. In a Christian wedding, the vows are distinctly Christian and only Christians are able to grasp the depth of those vows and be effective as witnesses. Only Christians can discern and encourage and if necessary, confront breaches of the wedding vows that Christians make.

Many people think that a Christian wedding is one conducted in a church by a preacher. It should be obvious that a Christian wedding is more about truth, faith and faithfulness than about the location. Of course unbelievers do not understand this. Unfortunately, many who call themselves Christians do not understand this either.

The Attitudes in Weddings

As mentioned earlier, weddings can be a source of tension, strife and conflict. Underlying the specifics of these troubles are often attitudes that are sinful, self-centered, lacking in love, and generally inconsiderate of others. Consider these attitudes that cause problems:

"It is **My** Wedding": Instead of having a biblical view of marriage, many people, especially brides, have a romantic princess attitude about the wedding. The wedding is viewed from a fairy-tale perspective: it is my wedding, and it is my special day so I will do what I want and I will get my way no matter what anyone else wants. This attitude not only results in making a major deal about minor things, it also violates basic tenants of the Christian faith. Christlike love is sacrificial, considering others more important than self.[178]

Brides are not the only ones who have a self-centered attitude associated with weddings. Many family members on all sides think that the wedding should be done their way and that everyone else should bow to them. The more people with this attitude, the more and greater the conflicts will be.

"There **are** Traditions": Most of what is done at weddings is based on traditions. Traditions vary. Traditions change. People involved in weddings tend to have very strong opinions about wedding traditions. They easily get offended when a tradition is neglected or broken or varied. Traditions are associated with invitations, wedding announcements, music, attire, flowers, order of service, seating locations, processions, exit, cakes, opening gifts, decorating the cake, the car, and . . .

---

178 Philippians 2:3-5 Do nothing from selfishness or empty conceit, but with humility of mind regard one another as more important than yourselves; do not merely look out for your own personal interests, but also for the interests of others. Have this attitude in yourselves which was also in Christ Jesus,

The problem is usually not with the tradition itself. The problem arises from the expectation, and insistence, that a particular tradition be followed. A felt need to have strict adherence to one set of traditions by one party and to a different set of traditions by another party is a train crash waiting to happen.

As unromantic as it may seem, weddings can be thoroughly Christian, completely functional, and greatly glorify God without most of the traditions often associated with weddings. Conversely, selfishly expecting and demanding conformance to traditions often needlessly hurts feelings and dishonors God. Weddings become a grievous drudgery rather than a joyous celebration of worship when sinful attitudes are present. Instead of reveling in God's creation, the wonder of marriage, and the blessing it is, people focus on how the wedding was not "done right," which is defined by their personal expectation related to tradition.

A Christian bride and groom may recognize the spiritual significance of the marriage ceremony. They may even say that honoring Christ is most important. Yet, the focus on and fights over traditions make the wedding something displeasing to God no matter what words are said.

"It Has to be Perfect": The verse in the Bible that says ". . . man looks at the outward appearance, but the LORD looks at the heart"[179] needs to be given careful consideration in weddings. Arising from the "princess for a day" idea is societal pressure to make the wedding an extravaganza of perfection. Usually folks settle for "at least putting on the best show we can afford" for the sake of appearances.

Often, most of the time spent planning and preparing for a wedding is about making sure everything is just right. The right dress, matching bridesmaid dresses, tuxes, shoes, flowers, candles, cakes, etc. Much of what is done is for show. Much of what is done is supposed to make the bride, the groom, the parents, the guests, feel special and important. Yet, seldom is anyone impressed with all the trappings. Instead of feeling special, all the fretting and fussing makes for an exhausted and frustrated bride on her wedding day. Stress over insignificant things is often shared by a number of people. Exiting newlyweds often is accompanied by a deep sigh, "I am glad that is over."

"Spare No Expense": Desiring to have the perfect wedding, being compelled to comply with traditions, and wanting to impress people are all very expensive. The average cost of a wedding today is conservatively estimated to be over $10,000 and frequently cited as well over $20,000. This financial burden adds to the stress of everyone. The expectation that things be done a certain way puts pressure on those expected (according to tradition) to pay. Often it would be better to have fewer expectations, fewer expenses and less inter-relational pressure. In many instances, the money spent on the wedding could be considered frivolous. After

179 1 Samuel 16:7

the wedding, there is little or even nothing to show for all that money. It would be appropriate to question whether weddings need all these things and whether spending money on these things is wise stewardship.

The wedding day is a very special occasion. Unfortunately, the preciousness of the occasion is often expressed through wrong, inappropriate and distorted attitudes. Many "essentials" aren't needed at all. Others things distract from or trivialize what is most important. Most significantly, relationships become strained or damaged when pride and selfishness exist. God looks for beauty, love, peace and humility in the heart; man looks on the outside. Many weddings sacrifice the traits God desires for the sake of the external trappings associated with the event.

There are certain functions that a wedding must accomplish. But most of what happens in a wedding has little to do with the real function of the wedding. Most wedding are more about tradition and extra-biblical expectations that actually detract from their main purpose. So, what is actually required to be part of the wedding according to the Bible?

Biblical Requirements for Weddings?

It may seem odd, but the biblical requirements for what a wedding should include are very simple. The wedding provides a way to join two people together as man and wife. The wedding provides a way for other people to know that the couple are married. That is it! Exactly how these things are accomplished is more an expression of tradition, culture and civil law. However, many of the things included in marriages often have some relationship to the Bible and what marriage is.

Wedding Practices with a Biblical Connection

Although, very few things are actually required for a wedding to be biblical, there are wedding practices that have some basis in or relationship to what the Bible teaches about marriage. These representations are often done out of tradition rather than out of a commitment to God and His Word. However, they can be very meaningful if their biblical significance is understood, communicated and embraced in the heart.

- Father giving away the bride – Although it is not politically correct, biblically, a daughter is under her father's authority until she marries.[180] At the wedding, the father transfers his authority over the daughter to the man becoming her husband.
- Rings – The giving of rings serves two Bible related functions. The ring is "unending" and symbolizes the nature of marriage as being lifelong. Also,

180 Numbers 30:3-13 makes this clear regarding vows made by a woman. First her father and then her husband, has veto power over any vow she might make.

172

the ring is a statement of the marriage commitment to everyone who sees it. The exclusiveness of the marriage relationship is announced to everyone who sees the ring.

- Unity Candles – The wedding is the transition for two people to become joined into one. The two lit candles at the beginning of the wedding symbolize their two separate lives. The lighting of the single candle and the extinguishing of the two symbolize that they are no longer two, but one. When the two families serve to light and extinguish the candles, there is also the representation that the man is leaving his father and mother and cleaving to his wife.

- Pronouncement – When it is announced that the two are now "man and wife," it is a public declaration that vows have been made and that the two are married. This emphasizes that exclusive rights and responsibilities are shared between the two, which should not be violated. It is now appropriate that the two be sexually intimate and it is wrong for them to be intimate with any other.

- Permission to kiss the bride – There is the assumption behind this permission that prior to this time, there has not been intimate physical contact. Kissing the bride usually follows immediately after the proclamation of being man and wife. Giving permission to kiss the bride is fairly meaningless if the two have been kissing previously, and especially if they have been sexually intimate.

Weddings may include other aspects that have some relationship with the biblical teachings about marriage. The significance of each of these depends upon knowing the underlying biblical teaching, making it known, and embracing it in the heart. Doing anything simply because it is tradition has little value.

Biblical Engagements

The Bible does not provide specific instructions regarding the engagement period of those who have agreed to be married. There are some examples of betrothals which provide the closest biblical parallel to engagements. Betrothals included three stages: agreement by families, public announcement, and the marriage ceremony. Engagements today are often much less weighty than betrothals were. The betrothal was legally binding. Only death (or legal divorce) could break it. Betrothals were often made by families, independent of those who would be married. This was because often those being betrothed were very young, years away from marrying age. The differences between engagements and betrothals more numerous than the similarities. Both do include a period of time between the agreement to be married and the marriage ceremony.

Some suggest that the engagement period allows people to really get to know their future spouse and to make sure that their decision to marry them is right. This perspective is based on the common practices of inadequate dating and premature consent to marry. No proposal, nor any acceptance of a proposal, should occur unless the other person is known well enough.

If two people are ready to marry, date in order to identify an appropriate future spouse, and agree it is right to marry each another, then what is the purpose of the engagement? How long of an engagement is appropriate?

Engagement periods should only as long as needed to prepare for the marriage ceremony and to make minimal preparations for married life. Often, wedding dates are delayed because of marriage ceremony traditions and cultural expectations associated with the wedding. If the wedding is viewed from its biblically defined function rather than from a "frills and fluff" standpoint, much less time is required to prepare.

Engagement periods may, and should, include time to complete a course in premarital counseling. Prior to agreeing to marry, couples should already understand much about their future spouse and about what marriage entails. However, it is usually very beneficial to complete premarital counseling with a pastor or a godly couple, who have significant life experience and deep biblical knowledge.

Engagements provide time to arrange for the practical aspects of the transition from being single to being married. This may include housing, transportation, relocation, etc.

Engagement – Elevated Temptations

Another factor to consider in engagement is the potential for an elevated level of temptation. Engaged people have, in some ways, already committed themselves to lifelong marriage to this specific person. It is easy to rationalize that the only thing between them and marriage is a ceremony and a piece of paper. This situation causes many people to wrongly think that they are "already married in God's eyes," and therefore sexual intimacy is acceptable. Additionally, engagements often include significant periods of private time between the couple. This also increases temptations. Purposeful care needs to be exercised to guard against crossing boundaries God establishes. Long engagements often increase the challenges in these areas.

Let's Celebrate Together

Marriage ceremonies, especially those of Christians, should be a cause of celebration, joy and the sharing of joy. Although some of what preceded in this chapter may have seemed to have had a kill-joy tone, the intent has been exactly the opposite. It is the wrong attitudes, the wrong focus, and wrong priorities in weddings that steal the joy from the occasion. There is cause for great joy when the marriage ceremony focuses on the Creator of marriage, the nature of marriage, and the blessing of marriage.

Joy in marriage comes from two people being joined together in a relationship that God created and declared to be very good. God said it is not good for man to be alone. In marriage, the "aloneness" is gone; and it is very good. Although there will be struggles because of sin in the world, the blessings of marriage far outweigh them if God is at the center of the relationship.

Those who are witnessing the wedding have opportunity to rejoice with those who are being married. This joy comes from knowing the potential blessing associated with marriage. For those who have good marriages themselves, it also provides an opportunity to rejoice in their own blessings. Those who are unmarried too can rejoice and anticipate the possibility that God may have for themselves in the future. For those who may be struggling in their marriage, the gospel presentation and a biblical presentation of marriage provide the opportunity for them to trust in Jesus and experience marriage as God designed and intended.

There is also rejoicing because marriage pictures a person's relationship with God. The union of marriage, including the love and submission, is a picture of God's relationship with His people. God sacrificially loved the world, proposed to those who would believe in Him and brings them into the blessing of His love. Each wedding is a reminder of God's love and the eternal blessing in Christ Jesus for everyone who believes.

Marriage ceremonies are important and necessary. They provide a clear transition point between being single and being married. They are necessary for legal reasons, and they serve a significant cultural function. They also are an occasion for celebrating the blessing of love between two people and between God and His people. Focusing on God's intent for marriage and the true meaning of marriage makes weddings a blessed event for everyone.

APPENDIX A: Study Questions

Chapter 1 – Origin and Definition of Marriage

1. Where did your idea of dating originate?
2. Where did your idea of marriage originate?
3. What is marriage?
4. How did marriage originate?
5. When should two people get married?
6. What percentage of marriages end in divorce?
7. What makes two people "compatible" to be married?
8. What does the Bible say makes two people "compatible"?
9. What role does love play in two people deciding to marry?
10. What does it mean for a husband to "cleave" to his wife?
11. What role do parents play in the lives of married children?
12. In what way is the image of God reflected in marriage?

Chapter 2 – Assumptions and Dating

1. When should a Christian begin dating? What age? What stage of life?
2. What is the origin of dating?
3. Explain where your understanding of dating originated. From parents teaching? From studying the Bible? From reading books? From TV, movies, etc.?
4. What happens on dates?
5. What does the Bible say about dating? List references.

Chapter 3 - Defining Dating
1. What is a date?
2. Why would someone date?
3. Why would someone not date?
4. Who dates?
5. What is the purpose of dating in the world?
6. What is the purpose of dating for the Christian?

Chapter 4 - Principles for Dating

1. Explain why typical dating does a fairly poor job of actually getting to know the other person.
2. What do people do in dating that is deceptive and hides who they really are?
3. Why do emotional attachments occur in dating?
4. What problems can emotional attachments lead to while dating and how do they prevent accomplishing the purpose of dating?
5. How does dating lead to problems with physical contact?

6. How can a person prevent problems with inappropriate physical contact in dating?
7. If you know that a person is someone you would not want to marry, then what does that mean regarding dating them?
8. Who is "eligible" for a Christian to marry?
9. What does it mean to be a Christian?
10. If a person says they are a Christian, does that mean they are a Christian?
11. What are some "red flags" in a potential date?
12. What are some "green flags" in a potential date?
13. What is a "predating deception removal discussion" and what should it include?
14. T F Sexual activity during dating is okay as long as you do not go "all the way."
15. T F Men and Women generally understand and appreciate how the other will respond in a dating relationship.
16. T F Parents are a good sounding board when considering whether or not to date someone.
17. T F If someone is not considered an eligible marriage partner, then one should not date that person.
18. T F People on dates often try to present themselves in a way that makes them appear better than they really are.
19. T F God approves of dating.

Chapter 5 - Choosing the Right Mate/Match

1. T F Dating is a good way to get to know someone well.
2. T F How people get along on dates is a good indication of how they will get along once married.
3. How can you really get to know the person you are dating?
4. What resources are available to learn about the person you are dating?
5. What is compatibility?
6. What constitutes compatibility for the Christian?
7. List and describe the different cultural preferences and barriers as they relate to future potential spouses.
8. How does dating contribute to or hinder finding the right mate?

Chapter 6 - Attraction, Modesty and Flirting

1. What is flirting?
2. Explain why something not intended to be flirting by one person is considered to be flirting by another person.
3. List some of the actions that may be flirting.
4. Is it right or wrong to flirt? Explain
5. Define "modesty."
6. Where in the Bible does it require modesty?
7. How does the Bible define modesty?

8. How is modesty related to humility and submission?
9. What does the term "sexy" mean and how does it relate to modesty?
10. Define "attractiveness."
11. Contrast the world's idea of attractiveness with God's view of attractiveness.
12. How do the different stages in life relate to do with one's perspective on flirting and attractiveness?

Chapter 7 Singleness - Unhindered Service

1. Is being single for all of one's life a good or bad thing?
2. Who should be content to be single?
3. When is singleness better than being married?
4. Under what circumstances does the Bible tell people to marry?
5. In what ways is marriage a distraction to serving the Lord?
6. Is being single more spiritual than being married?
7. What does the Bible say about prohibiting marriage?

Chapter 8 – Divorce: perspective on biblical teaching

1. What is marriage?
2. What percentage of marriages end in divorce?
3. When is the best time to learn what God says about divorce?
4. Who wins when two people divorce?
5. List all of the reasons people think God allows couples to get a divorce.
6. Explain how the initial assumptions and initial questions about divorce change the conclusions that are reached.
7. How does a person's understanding of marriage alter how one views divorce?
8. What does the Bible say about taking another believer to court?
9. What would likely be the church's position on divorce if it were not so prevalent?
10. What is the relationship between forgiveness and divorce?
11. Explain what Jesus said about adultery and the implications it has on the issue of divorce?
12. Is the basis for divorce the same for remarriage? Explain.

Chapter 9 – Communication: To Speak or Not to Speak

1. How would you define effective communication?
2. What are some barriers to effective communication?
3. How does familiarity hinder effective communication?
4. List and discuss the six steps in effective communication.
5. What is "feedback" in the communication process?
6. What role does poor communication play in creating conflicts in marriage?

7. Who is responsible if poor communication occurs?
8. List five commands that the Bible gives regarding communication.
9. T F The better you know someone the less likely you will have poor communication.

Chapter 10 – Wives: How to Be a Godly One

1. What was the wife's role when God created her?
2. How did the wife's role change after sin entered the world?
3. Is submission part of the creation design or the effect of sin?
4. In what ways do wives seek to assume the role of the husband?
5. What did God mean when He said the woman's "desire would be for her husband"?
6. What happens when two people are both "the boss"?
7. Are women commanded to love their husbands? In what way?
8. In what way is the wife's role like the church's relationship to Christ?
9. How does a wife's responsibility change when her husband is unbelieving?
10. When is a wife not to submit to her husband?

Chapter 11 – Husbands: How to be a Godly One

1. According to husbands, which spouse is the cause of most marital problems?
2. What are two extremes that husbands are to avoid in marriage?
3. What changed in the roles of men and women after the fall?
4. Is domination by the man a result of creation or a result of sin?
5. What term is used in the Bible to describe the husband's relationship to his wife?
6. What is the husband's responsibility toward his wife?
7. How does marriage correspond to the church's relationship with Christ?
8. How much is the husband to sacrifice for the sake of his wife?
9. In what way is a husband to grant honor to his wife?
10. Is there any way in which a husband is "better" than his wife?

Chapter 12 - Children: Burden or Blessing?

1. What does the Bible say about children being a blessing?
2. What does the Bible say about birth control?
3. For what reasons do people limit the size of their families?
4. Which of the above reasons have a biblical basis and which are selfish?
5. What role did children have in God blessing Israel?
6. If one followed the Old Testament law regarding sexual relations in marriage would they have many or few children?
7. What changed in child bearing as a result of the fall?
8. List the reasons why people have abortions. Now list the reasons why people practice birth control. Compare and contrast the two lists.

9. What is the relationship between parenting and discipleship?
10. What is the goal of parenting?

Chapter 13 - Money and Debt: Gravel in the Gears of Marriage

1. Which of your views on finances are the result of biblical teaching and which ones are the result of "observation?"
2. What percentage of what is "yours" belongs to God?
3. What needs does God promise to meet?
4. What is the "American Dream," and how much of that has God promised us?
5. Is it harder for God to give us a million dollars or a nickel?
6. What is the relationship between contentment and borrowing?
7. What is the relationship between patience and borrowing?
8. Is borrowing trusting God or testing God? How?
9. How would you define "stewardship?"
10. When should a Christian give, and when should they loan?
11. Describe how a budget can help eliminate marriage conflict.

Chapter 14 – Sharing Responsibilities: Who is Doing What?

1. What household jobs belong to wives?
2. What household jobs are the husband's responsibility?
3. What has determined how you answered the above two questions?
4. How can couples minimize conflict regarding division of duties?
5. Who will set the expectations you will have for what your spouse will do?

Chapter 15 - Conflict Resolution: Seeking Peace, not Victory

1. How often do you expect to have a conflict with your spouse?
2. List potential sources of conflict within marriage.
3. In your opinion, how much conflict springs from poor communication?
4. How can the significance and duration of conflict be minimized?
5. Describe the role that each of the following play in preventing and correcting conflict:
    a) Submission to authority (human and God's)
    b) Humility (What is humility?)
    c) Forgiveness (What is forgiveness?)
    d) Love
6. How soon should conflicts be resolved?
7. Who is responsible to initiate resolution of conflicts?

Chapter 16 – Sex: The Big Picture Perspective

1. When does a person need to learn about the intimate details of sex?
2. What role does sex have in marriage?

3. What role does sex have outside of marriage?
4. What purpose does sex have?
5. What are the basic differences in men and women regarding sexual satisfaction?
6. How important is one's emotional state to sexual satisfaction? (For men? For women?)
7. Who owns the Christian's body?
8. When is it appropriate to abstain from sex?

Chapter 17 – Companionship: Being Best Friends

1. How would you define a "friend"?
2. How do people become friends?
3. If marriage partners are not friends, then what are they?
4. What are some ways in which friendships are fostered?
5. What is the relationship between friendship and shared interests?
6. Is it possible to spend time together without spending time together? Explain and give examples.
7. Which does cultivation of friendship require more of, thoughtfulness or money? Why?

Chapter 18 - How to Find a Husband or Wife

1. How much experience does a young person have in finding a mate when they reach the stage of being ready to marry?
2. Why would a young person who is desiring to be married be hesitant to admit it to anyone?
3. What are challenges when trying to find a spouse?
4. What special challenges do committed Christians face?
5. List and explain the resources available to the Christian young person who is open to being married.
6. Discuss the significance of location regarding potential spouses.
7. Explain the balance between trusting God, being available and taking some action to find a spouse.

Chapter 19 - The Wedding

1. List the things that are typically included in a wedding.
2. What is legally required to be in a wedding?
3. What does God require to be in a wedding?
4. List and explain the things in weddings that have some biblical significance related to marriage.
5. Discuss whether a wedding is required in order to be married.
6. Identify those things that make a wedding distinctively Christian.
7. What should be the Christian attitude toward weddings for the different people who may be involved?

8. List and explain attitudes that can hijack the wedding.
9. Discuss engagements: the purpose, dangers and an appropriate length.
10. Discuss the celebratory nature of weddings and how an atmosphere of joy can be established and maintained.

APPENDIX B: - Personal Financial Testimony
"God Never Promised Me a House!"

Looking back with my wife over three decades of marriage and parenting there have been many important decisions in our lives. Two of those decisions stand out above all others. One was the decision to not have a TV in our home from the time our first child was on the way. The second life-changing decision is the focus of this appendix - to become debt free and to remain free of debt regardless of the cost. Both of these decisions were based upon biblical convictions about what constitutes God's best for His children. At the time of the second edition of this book, we have maintained those decisions.[181]

Submission – The Foundation

In the fly leaf of my old Bible is recorded a commitment that Mary and I made individually on May 17, 1981. It reads in part "Dedication of my life to the stewardship of the Lord. Time, talents and treasures . . ."

That was a sincere commitment. It seemed to mark the beginning of a new phase of our life journey. It was a foundational commitment that significantly influenced many major decisions that have brought us to where we are today. Full submission to God and His Word became the basis for submitting to Him on such a difficult matter as to how we should view and handle money. Absent that wholesale submission to God, it is likely that many other specific decisions would have been made without submission.

Wrestling with Trusting God

In 1983, I set my mind to study what the Scripture had to say about finances. We had been to a seminar, and I was using some printed material obtained there to point me to some of the biblical texts that address money. I had many questions about money. This caused me to dig deeper and deeper, reading and cross referencing every text that seemed to touch on finances.

It was during this study that I first came to the conclusion that it was not best for Christians to be in debt. For us personally, my conviction became that it was a sin for us to be in debt. After I shared my conclusions with my wife, together we made a commitment to get out of debt in five years. A written plan captured our intent to get out of debt. The plan was based on the good paying job I had, making only necessary expenditures, and the amount we were in debt. We had been married three years and owed $55,000 on our house mortgage plus $15,000 on 40 acres that I had begun to buy before our marriage. The plan seemed realistic. Assuming all went well, we could be debt free in five years. There was a

---

181 Now that our children are grown, we view television some at grandma's house, which is adjacent to our home.

peace and comfort knowing that we were taking specific steps to honor God with how we used the money he gave us. But that peace was soon to be shattered.

I continued to study what the Bible had to say about finances. The decision to get out of debt was based on trusting God to give us what we needed when we needed it. It was based on allowing Him to guide our lives by providing or withholding financial resources according to His will. It was based on a willingness to be patient and wait for God. It was based on being free to serve God rather than being a slave to those to whom we owed money.[182]

In addition to studying finances, I was memorizing Romans 6. I would rehearse the verses in my mind or say them aloud while driving or working. Soon after our five year plan was in place the reciting of these verses while splitting fire wood became the occasion for a life changing encounter with God. The verses ran through my mind as I chopped the wood.

> What shall we say then? Are we to continue in sin that grace might increase? May it never be! How shall we who died to sin still live in it? (Romans 6:1-2)

I have never heard God audibly speak. But on that day, I am sure that the thoughts in my mind were prompted by His Spirit. They rang in my head like the echo of a school bell. God said to my heart, "If you think it is not best for a Christian to be in debt (and a sin for you) why wait five years to get out of debt?"

It was a question of submission and commitment. It was a question of conviction. It was a question of sacrifice. I had become fully convinced that it was not best for God's people to be in debt. Actually, for me personally, I was convinced that borrowing money was a lack of faith in God, and therefore, sinful. (Intent on not holding others to my convictions, I prefer to say that it is not best to be in debt.)

Now I was challenged with obeying God immediately rather than delaying to do what I was convinced is God's best. I had a hard choice to make. Putting down my splitting hammer and wedges, I slowly climbed the steep bank leading to our home. My thoughts were clear, but I was dazed. It was as if I had hit myself in the head with the hammer. I called Mary. I said we needed to talk. We sat on the porch, and an air of seriousness settled. I told her. She wept. "This is happening too fast," she pleaded.

Soon we agreed and changed our previous plans. We embraced a decision to get out of debt as soon as possible rather than in the next five years. The air cleared. The load of bricks lifted. Peace filled our hearts. Before us lay a long hard road requiring the elimination of $70,000 of debt as soon as possible. But a calm reserve overwhelmed our souls.

---

182 The scriptural basis for these principles is laid out in Chapter 10.

After the decision to get out of debt was solidified, something else began to happen. My heart began to long to go to Bible college. The seed of this desire had been planted in me a couple years earlier but had fallen into remission, perhaps because of work, children, establishing a home and life in general. Now it floated on the surface of my thinking like a piece of unsinkable Styrofoam. I fought with myself. I was afraid to mention it to Mary, my wife. I "knew" in my male-sort-of-way that she could not handle this too. Finally, after a couple of weeks when the desire had not subsided, I sheepishly broached the subject. I braced for the flood of emotions and potential backlash as I revealed I would like to go to Bible college. With almost no discussion she said something like, "I think that is a good idea." I was floored by how easily she accepted the idea.

We were pumped! We were excited about what God had shown us about finances. We were thrilled by what God was showing us and by the decisions we were making. But our enthusiasm was met with lukewarm responses at best. Friends, family and even the church seemed to view us as fanatical and extreme. In our joy we shared enthusiastically with people who said they were committed to the same God we serve and the same Bible we read. But people's responses frequently left us with the impression that they felt that our actions were a judgment on them.

Innumerable times people said, "You will never own a house if you do not go in debt."[183] After getting over the initial shock of how people responded, my reply became very simple, "God never promised that I would own a house. He has promised to meet my needs day by day." We were not deserted, but we did feel somewhat alienated. We were not alone, for God was with us. We were convinced we were doing what was right.

With a commitment to get out of debt and to go to Bible college we set to work. We put our house up for sale. We listed it for the equity we had invested in it. It did not sell. The early 1980's housing market was in a slump. Willing to do whatever it took to get out of debt as soon as possible, we soon lowered our price to the amount we had paid for the house. It did not sell. Before long we lowered the asking price to the balance on the mortgage. It did not sell. To get out of debt as soon as possible, we decided it best to give the house back to the people from whom we were buying it. This would require us to take a financial loss of about $10,000. This was the result of making extra mortgage principal payments and improvements we had made to the property.

At each step of the process, we had informed the owners of our actions and intent. They were not particularly happy with us. They would have preferred to continue to get monthly mortgage payments instead of regaining ownership of the home (especially during the housing downturn). But in this too, God seemed to be at work. The mortgage holders were associated with a religious organization that promoted works as a means of salvation. Near the end of this process, the

---

183 Since then, we have owned five houses without going into debt.

woman visited us. She said, "You are such good people. You are better than us." In short, she wanted us to become members of their group. Although her logic eluded us, God showed us that giving the house back had not been a blight on our testimony for Him.

In October of 1983, we traveled to the title company. We signed the papers. Our creditors signed the papers. The papers were notarized. We paid the required $35 fee. They took the house back including our investments of time, labor and money. We were relieved and closer to being debt free. We felt that God was pleased.

We soon began to notice unusual things, things that were not "normal." They were blessings from God in our lives, and these were assisting us in reaching our goal of being debt free. We found a place to rent just down the road from where we had lived. The rent was inexpensive. The Christian landlord, for no apparent reason, lowered the rent shortly after we moved in. Additionally, he provided us with free firewood for the winter. Actually, the landlord had bought our excess firewood when we moved out of our other house. Now, after we had received the money for the wood, we were burning it for free in our new home. These blessings served to help us toward our goal of getting out of debt.

At the job upon which our initial "get out of debt in five years plan" was based, a strike seemed to be imminent. Having been compelled to be a member of the union in order to work there, I now had to personally struggle with all of the associated issues. Do I work for the company or for the union? What should I do if there is a strike? It seemed that a strike would be contrary to achieving our debt-free goal. We watched and waited, trusting God's will to be done. We remained committed to getting out of debt as soon as possible. The union vote was finally taken, and the strike averted. This was good news and a big relief. Part of the relief was that I could continue to work without having to choose between loyalty to the company or to the union.

Surprisingly, the union had settled for a three-year wage freeze. That was fine with me. I did not want to deal with a strike. Then God surprised us again. Within two weeks, while doing the exact same job, I received a two dollar an hour pay raise. Through some administrative changes my job was reclassified and I received this increase. This change affected fewer than 10 people in a company with hundreds of employees. I was one of them. The additional pay would go toward paying off the remaining debt owed on the 40 acres. At the same time, we were trying to sell that property. But the economy and market were so poor that there was no interest in it.

Next came the opportunity to work on a special crew at my job. This would require me to work much overtime. After discussing it with Mary and my pastor, I decided to join the crew. The extra pay proved very helpful in retiring the debt.

By August 1984, ten months after the "get out of debt a.s.a.p." decision, we were debt free. The house was gone and the land was paid for. We had also saved ~$8,000 for school. We had chosen a school in Canada. It was a doctrinally sound school, but the cost of tuition was less than half that of an equivalent Bible college in the USA.

Being a U.S. Navy veteran, I was able to draw money from the G.I. bill. We had been told by one "in the know"[184] that we would not be able to live on the relatively small amount that would be available to us. We had two small children, but we were undaunted. We were willing to trust God. He proved much more trustworthy than our feeble faith warranted.

After arriving in Canada the exchange rate soared to unprecedented heights. Our American dollar became worth $1.53 Canadian. All of our funds were in American dollars. All expenses were in Canadian dollars. Not only that, but also, our rent was cheap, $200/month Canadian, including all utilities. We were not able to work in Canada; but were covered by their social medicine, and all our medical expenses were fully paid.[185]

I finished a four year program in three years by taking a heavy load and some summer courses. By graduation in the spring of 1987 I had only worked for pay for about one and one half months. Amazingly, we still had a significant portion of that original $8,000 left, even though we had, by necessity, traded cars twice.

After graduation, we accepted a call to a new church in Maui. Since the church was small and not well established, we paid our own expenses to move. We reduced our worldly possessions to fit into an air cargo container measuring 4 feet by 4 feet by 5 feet.

Hawaii is another long story of God's work and faithfulness in our lives, but we were not able to stay there.By February 1988 after making the return trip and paying required taxes, our funds were completely depleted. We had the rent paid for the month. We had some used furniture, a 1978 VW van, three small children, and nothing but a promise of my old job. We had no savings, no retirement funds, no life insurance, nothing. The church which we were attending at the time was sensitive to our situation and gave us a monetary gift. Otherwise we would have been asking for food.

The job that I had been promised was to start the first of the year. The first of the year came and went, but no job. Although it was stretching for us, we eventually realized that the delay in employment was in control of a good God. The promised job included a rotating shift work schedule. The delay in getting the job

---

184 This was a friend who worked at a local college finance dept. She was an unbeliever at the time but has since been saved.

185 I am not a proponent of social medicine, but it adequately served us then.

allowed for me to apply for, and obtain, a different job, with all day-time hours and a higher salary. The delay in the promised job was God working for our good, even though it was not apparent until later. Having waited and obtaining this job instead of the promised one allowed me to regularly teach Sunday School and mid-week Bible studies. On February 11, 1988, I went back to work.

About a year later we became acquainted with a woman who had received an old house as part of an estate. The house was in very poor shape. She intended to fix the house for her daughter. However, the high cost of estimated repairs caused her to have second thoughts. Some contractors told her that it would be better to demolish the existing structure and start from scratch.

Mary and I were not opposed to renting, but we preferred to make better use of our money if possible. Our commitment to remain debt free never wavered. So, I approached this woman with a proposal. I suggested that we lease the house with an option to buy. The lease payment could be made either in cash payments or in cash receipts of equal or greater value for materials purchased for improvement of the home. While the offer was not totally ridiculous, it was on the verge of being so. The woman may or may not have been offended by the offer, but she said she would never be willing to consider such a proposal.

The phone rang about a month later. The woman had a change of heart. Now she wanted to discuss the proposal and asked that I resubmit it to her. I drafted the main aspects, and she had her attorney draw up the paperwork. The final agreement was identical to what I had proposed the first time. In essence, the lease was a glorified rental agreement with unusual terms. The terms included a fixed value of the home and a very low monthly lease payment (about half of what we had been paying for rent). Upon signing the paperwork, the woman's husband commented, "Call me if you need a match to torch the place." Indeed, it was not the best house by modern standards; but it was, or at least soon would be, habitable.

Over the next two years, all of the lease money was invested directly into the home. There was no exchange of funds with the home owner. We did all of the work ourselves, including roofing, wiring, windows, landscaping, pruning and carpeting.

Mary had always wanted to have an antique-collectibles shop. After obtaining permission from our landlord and a conditional use permit from the county, the detached garage was converted into a small cozy store for her. Now our home had also allowed for turning her beloved hobby into a small business venture.

Upon the completion of the second year of the lease, we paid cash to purchase the home, paying in full the agreed upon price. God had blessed us. We owned a house. We had not borrowed to do it. God had given me a good paying job, we had no rent, and we had only had a minimal monthly lease investment. In this way, we were able to save enough money to buy the house for the low amount previously designated. We were now home owners. "It could never be done without going into debt," we had been told. God proved them to be wrong ,and we rejoiced in Him.

The 40 acres of investment property which we had tried to sell when getting out of debt was on the market again. We had tried to sell it several times before, and thought we had it sold at least once. Apparently, God had other plans. Now there were three buyers who were bidding on the property. Shortly before we bought our house, we accepted an offer on the property for a full fifteen percent more than our asking price. We were stunned and certainly pleased. This money was not needed now. We had thought many times before that we needed the money but God knew better than we did, what we did and did not need.[186]

Mary and I had been involved in nursing home ministries of one sort or another for many years. At this time we began to consider the possibility of starting a senior foster care home to give a few of these elderly people a better place to live. This interest, although never fully materialized, resulted in our inquiry about large homes in the area, and especially older ones.

In a town a few miles from where we lived at that time, was a very large old house. It had a long history in the community, which included a popular restaurant. Unfortunately, over the previous decade, the house had experienced much misfortune. Bankruptcy by the owners, an IRS auction, and most recently a fire, had left the building on the brink of demolition. It hung sadly on the embankment overlooking the highway, windows broken, stained by smoke and draped with a blue tarp. Mary and I would jest with one another as we drove by saying, "Hey, maybe we ought to buy that place." The thought seemed ludicrous on all counts. But God does have a sense of humor. The joke was on us as God's blessings continued.

We eventually made an offer on the house based on the funds we had available. That offer was rejected. Then we decided that we would sell our current house and buy the big house if all the pieces fell into place. We made the offer on the big house contingent on the sale of our house. The offer was accepted. We listed our house for sale on Saturday, contingent on the purchase of the big house. By Monday we had a full price offer. Through an oversight, the contingency was not included in our sale agreement; and we did not catch it. As the closing date on the sale of our house approached, it was revealed that there existed about $45,000 in liens on the big house. We were befuddled. Our house was sold. The other house seemed to be slipping away. We knew we were moving, but we were not sure where.

---

186 It should be mentioned that the purchase of the 40 acres was not a "good" investment. We would have been better off to have put the money we put into it in the bank at low or even no interest.

During the three years since we had left the ministry in Hawaii, I was active in ministry teaching Sunday School and Bible studies. Yet people would frequently ask if, or when, I would return to full-time ministry. Now with the sale of our house imminent and the purchase of this other one questionable, we concluded that God had decided it was time for us to move. Perhaps this was God's way of getting us to move where He wanted. In all this we were willing to go or do whatever God may have for us. Our preference would have been for Him to tell us in some other way though.

Somehow the bank was able to clear the liens on the big house. By February 1991, we had moved into the big house in spite of all its hurts. We had sold the fixed-up little house for enough money to buy the un-fixed big one. We had the money from the sale of the 40 acres to begin the repairs. Now, we owned our second house without going into debt.

Over the next year, we diligently worked to repair the building: heating, wiring, plumbing, framing, roofing, etc. I worked four 10-hour days at my job and two long days on the big house each week. Although we are not legalistic about it, we see wisdom in taking a day off each week. I seldom did any work on weeknights since we sought to maintain a proper balance with work and the family. By this time child number five was on the way. By March of 1992, we moved the family upstairs into our essentially "new" home, which previously was a blackened hulk.

Mary's parents had been living in a travel trailer and assisting during the reconstruction. When the major repairs were completed and we moved upstairs, they sold their own home and moved into part of the downstairs of the big house. One of the two outbuildings had served as Mary's store while construction progressed. Now the store moved into part of the ground floor of the main house. Work began to convert the outbuilding into an apartment for her mother and father.

Once that building was complete, the electrical generating facility at which I worked shut down permanently. I was laid off with a severance package. Out of a long-standing Bible study I had been leading for several years, we had started a church, which met in the "meeting room" in the big house. Prior to the plant shutdown, I had been negotiating with my supervisors about becoming a part-time employee so I could devote more time to ministry. These discussions were progressing well but were preempted by the layoff.

The severance money along with money we had saved, was used to purchase another run-down house as a rental. Now we owned our third house without going into debt.[187] Over the next few months this house was refurbished and rented. About this same time I accepted responsibility as pastor of a second small

---

187 It could be counted as our fourth house if the grandparents' house was included.

church about seventeen miles away. Staggered services and Sunday School times allowed me to preach at both church services.

In June of 1993, our 2-year-old daughter was diagnosed with type 1 Diabetes. This resulted in a new and rigid regimen in our lives that began to conflict with having the home and the business under the same roof. Her shot, snack and meal schedule needed to be closely followed. We did not have the same flexibility as before.

Also, our oldest son was five years old; and he began to cause me to remember my childhood in the country with lots of open space to run and explore. With the business and the traffic, it was hard to allow the children to play outside without constant supervision. By the spring of 1995, I had a desire to provide my children some of the benefits of country life that I enjoyed as a youngster. Mary was receptive to the idea.

We wanted to be out of town but have an easy commute for running the store and ministering to the churches. We wanted to have at least five acres so that there would be plenty of room for the kids to run and perhaps for animals too. But everything seemed so expensive.

We prayed and asked God to search our hearts. We had been so abundantly blessed. Were we being greedy? Were our motives right? We evaluated our resources and decided to liquidate some assets including the rental house and retirement accounts. Even with this, it was evident that any place we could find would be a stretch; and it would definitely have to be a "fixer upper." We now had some experience in fixing things up. Child number 7 was on the horizon.

After fruitless dealings with real estate agents, we ran an ad in the local paper. "Wanted: Older home on acreage in Rainier area." The response was not overwhelming but it did the job. Wednesday evening after Bible study the phone rang. A party was responding to our ad. We went to see. As we drove into the driveway, Mary and I looked at each other with common surprise on both of our faces. This was not the "fixer upper" that we had imagined. We toured the house, but darkness was approaching. We both agreed the price would likely be well above our reach.

The next day, I went for a more detailed look. By the time I left, a handshake agreement had been made with the property owners to "buy the farm." The property (14 acres with house, barn, garage and shed) was in a state of neglect but not great disrepair. An appointment with the home owner's lawyer could not be scheduled until Tuesday. The bargain price we had agreed upon caused us to wonder if the seller might back out in the interim. They honored the agreement and all went smoothly.

The purchase agreement was based on being able to sell our rental house. We had 3 months to find a buyer or the farm deal would fall through. The housing market was hot, so we listed it at the higher end. We had much interest but no buyer. One day, the phone rang; and a man asked if we would take a certain amount for the house. I said that we would, and they came right over. When they exited the car I recognized the man. He was previously a professor at Multnomah School of the Bible. I had met him the previous March at our IFCA Regional Conference. He was helping his son-in-law buy the house. The son-in-law had been hired by the local school district. Coincidence? Is there any such thing with God?

Throughout our life, our commitment to stay out of debt had been continuously tested. Now, however, an intense struggle began for me. I began to crunch the numbers. Since our tax laws are not conducive to doing business God's way, we were going to have to pay a large amount of our money from the sale of the rental house to the government. However, the tax liability could be greatly reduced by borrowing money for a short time. Instead, we decided that staying out of debt was the right thing. We bit the bitter bullet and paid the taxes ,trusting that God is in control and knows all these things.

In October 1995 we bought our fourth house without going into debt and moved our family to the country home. Before moving, we had been aware of some of the tension present in our previous living arrangement. Moving proved to be a good decision, as we found the family in a more relaxing environment. God is so good. Within a year, the farm was all fixed up and in a state of regular maintenance mode: new paint in and out, water line, plumbing, roofs, etc.

By 1997, the business had begun to demand more time and effort than we wanted to give. There was tension, not bad tension, but never-the-less tension about the priority of family, ministry, and business. By fall, we decided to close out the business and sell the commercial property. People would frequently inquire regarding our reasons for selling out. My response came to be "We are adjusting our activities to match our priorities."

Since the first edition of this book was completed, we have continued to trust God to lead us through our finances. The big house was sold on a 30 year contract, and, Lord willing, will provide financial resources to invest in the kingdom until Mary and I are well into our 70's. We now manage the original country home acreage for forest production. Additionally, God has provided financial resources to purchase two other small parcels of undeveloped forest land. For a while, we served three rural churches, but now we serve at one. Operating a portable sawmill and cutting some lumber from our own trees supplements the family's income.

We do not know what God has in store for the future. We do know, though, that God has proven Himself faithful. For us, His faithfulness has been manifested in both material and spiritual ways. Yet, we will continue to trust Him in abundance or poverty. We hold all that we have loosely, realizing that the Lord has given and the Lord may take away. Nevertheless, whatever may come we intend to echo the words of Job, "Naked I came from my mother's womb, And naked I shall return there. The LORD gave and the LORD has taken away. Blessed be the name of the LORD."[188]

No Magic Formulas

Whenever I share all or part of the above testimony, I always add a word of caution to those who may be looking for the magic formula for God's material blessing. Faith pleases God. Without faith it is impossible to please God.[189] However, God's blessing comes in many different forms and ways. He may bless materially, but the best blessings are spiritual. I tell people, "You may do exactly the same thing which Mary and I have done, and God may allow you to live in poverty all of the days of your life. You may have faith in God stronger than our faith and you may never own a thing. The purpose of our faith is not to gain God's blessing but rather to honor Him to the best of our knowledge and ability."

Furthermore, the above testimony is not intended to imply that we have some corner on the truth. Neither is it intended to imply that God's material blessings are the certain evidence of God's approval. Rather, the testimony is offered as an encouragement to step out in faith trusting God to provide for your needs. Do not be afraid to be different if you become convinced of something from the Word of God.

---

188 Job 1:21
189 Hebrews 11:6

ABOUT THE AUTHOR

Jeff Mullins is a tent making pastor serving in rural churches in Northwestern Oregon. For the past 25 years he has been actively involved in training men to carefully interpret the Bible and effectively preach, including six month long trips to conduct pastoral training in Russia and Africa.

Jeff has a great passion for God's Word and a fervor for careful interpretation and purposeful practical application.

Jeff is a member of the IFCA International and has served as a missionary pastor with Northwest Independent Church Extension (NICE). He has been serving at Canaan Community Church in Deer Island, Oregon, for over two decades.

Jeff has been married to Mary Mullins since 1979. They have seven children together, most of whom are actively involved in Christian service.

Jeff is the author of numerous magazine articles and two other books:

Good Sermon, Brother! (available in English, Swahili and Russian)

Children: Raising or Ruining?

Jeff operates Creation Woods (creationwoods.com), a portable sawmill business, to help support his family and to be able to contribute to missions work around the world.

Additional copies of this book and the author's other books are available at amazon.com.

Made in the USA
San Bernardino, CA
28 February 2018